Praise for *Parent Up*

"*Parent Up* is exactly the book parents need in our rapidly changing world. It reminds today's teachers, parents, and caregivers that leadership requires empathy, and the better we understand others, the better we understand ourselves."

—Michele Borba, EdD, author of *Unselfie: Why Empathetic Kids Succeed in Our All-About-Me World*

"Kelly Rippon's engaging book is about helping your children become the very best version of themselves—without forcing them to be somebody they're not... *Parent Up* gives parents the confidence to raise our children in a way that works for our families, and inspires resilience and self-sufficiency in our kids."

—Lindsay Powers, author of *You Can't F*ck Up Your Kids: A Judgment-Free Guide to Stress-Free Parenting*

"Kelly shares relatable personal experiences in *Parent Up* that show us sometimes the difficult path leads to the best parenting. Not always protecting our kids, but allowing them to own the consequences of their actions, helps them learn to be confident, empathetic, accountable, and ultimately empowered to live their best lives. It's no wonder her oldest son, Adam, achieved his Olympic dream and is a beloved sports figure."

—Kristi Yamaguchi, Olympic champion and *New York Times* bestselling author

"This book is a total joy! Kelly Rippon is a remarkable mother of six remarkable children whose achievements are only surpassed by their integrity and goodness of heart. Her book offers a wealth of advice for raising successful and compassionate children. Warm, witty, and wise, Kelly Rippon is a gift to all parents!"

—Priscilla Gilman, author of *The Anti-Romantic Child: A Story of Unexpected Joy*

"*Parent Up* is a must-read for parents and anyone with children in their life! Kelly Rippon offers practical strategies to create an environment that grows confidence, empathy, and kindness in kids, explaining the influences that allow them to become their authentic selves in an environment of unconditional love."

—Judy Shepard, author of *The Meaning of Matthew* and cofounder and president of the Matthew Shepard Foundation

"*Parent Up* is the perfect antidote to the never-enough mentality that weighs so many parents down. Combining an extraordinary gift of perspective with parenting stories from the front lines, Rippon delivers a step-by-step guide for how to ignite the best in yourself and your children at the same time."

—Katherine Wintsch, author of *Slay Like a Mother*

"Kelly Rippon speaks from the experience of raising six successful kids, including Olympic medalist Adam Rippon, as well as her work in corporate leadership coaching... *Parent Up* is filled with insights on how to raise children who believe in themselves and view the world with optimism, but it's also about a mother bursting with pride for her children, discovering the impact of her own actions, and eagerly sharing these insights with moms currently in the trenches so that we can one day feel the same."

—Ilana Wiles, author of *The Mommy Shorts Guide to Remarkably Average Parenting*

"As a mom of three, I can confidently say...I've never quite liked parenting books. That is, until *Parent Up*. I needed a book that spoke into raising kids in a way that felt good for me as a parent, bringing up individual humans, not just wild beings that needed managing. I loved Kelly's approach in ways that simplified things, like creating habits and boundaries versus just rules. It feels approachable, honest, and most of all, relatable. Parents really are their kid's first influencers, and this book really built up my confidence to be the best kind of influencer (not a controller) of my kids."

—Sarah Nicole Landry, The Birds Papaya

Parent Up

Inspire Your Child to Be Their Best Self

KELLY RIPPON

To my children, Adam, Tyler, Brady, Jordan, Dagny, and Sawyer

and to all the people in this world who take the

time to listen to others without judgment.

Published by Sourcebooks
P.O. Box 4410, Naperville, Illinois 60567-4410
(630) 961-3900
sourcebooks.com

Library of Congress Cataloging-in-Publication Data

Names: Rippon, Kelly, author.
Title: Parent up : inspire your child to be their best self / Kelly Rippon.
Description: Naperville : Sourcebooks, 2020.
Identifiers: LCCN 2020020041 (print) | LCCN 2020020042 (ebook)
Subjects: LCSH: Parenting. | Parent and child.
Classification: LCC HQ755.8 .R56 2020 (print) | LCC HQ755.8 (ebook) | DDC 649/.1--dc23
LC record available at https://lccn.loc.gov/2020020041
LC ebook record available at https://lccn.loc.gov/2020020042

Printed and bound in the United States of America.
VP 10 9 8 7 6 5 4 3 2 1

Contents

Foreword by Adam Rippon   vii

Introduction: Understanding Influence   xi

CHAPTER 1: The Influence of Optimism   1

CHAPTER 2: The Influence of Words   25

CHAPTER 3: The Influence of Perspective   49

CHAPTER 4: The Influence of Confidence   69

CHAPTER 5: The Influence of Empathy   87

CHAPTER 6: The Influence of Grace   103

CHAPTER 7: The Influence of Loyalty   121

CHAPTER 8: The Influence of Habits   137

CHAPTER 9: The Influence of Accountability   159

CHAPTER 10: The Influence of Kindness   175

Conclusion: Being Your Best Self   191

Acknowledgments   195

About the Author   198

Foreword

BY ADAM RIPPON

When I think of my mom, I think of someone who has always given selflessly. As I've gotten older and hit my thirties, I appreciate more and more of what she has given me and taught me. When your mom tells you to stay positive or to never give up, sometimes it can feel like, *Really, Mom?!* Of course your mom is going to say that!

A lot of the lessons I learned from my mom I didn't really understand until I was older. I didn't understand that so many of the habits I formed were because of her—I always heard what she was saying, but it wasn't until I was older that I was living by it. I was stubborn when I was young; I wanted things immediately, and I wanted to be perfect. It was a pressure I put on myself.

My mom always told me to watch the way I spoke to myself, that my brain was always listening. I didn't understand what she meant when she told me this at first. I thought that if I wasn't mean to myself, I wouldn't be able to get motivated. She told me to always watch the words I used. I knew it was important; I was very good at helping my friends through tough situations, and I would never accept them talking down to themselves. I eventually learned that if I wasn't going to allow my friends to speak to themselves that way, I shouldn't allow myself to talk to *me* that way.

Growing up, there were times I didn't believe in myself or in what I was doing. Performing and competing in a sport where you are constantly judged against your peers, I found it difficult at times to stay optimistic. I wanted so badly to be perfect. For years it held me back in my sports life. I knew I was capable of so much more than my results were showing and far more than I was telling myself in my lowest moments, the ones when I felt like quitting. I became more aware of what I was saying in my head and decided to make a change. I improved my self-talk, and I improved my results. I pushed myself further than I thought I could go, after I started telling myself that I was powerful. I forced myself to see the bigger picture. I didn't know where this inner voice came from that pushed me to get through those moments, but it was there. I didn't know until later that it came from my mom.

I wanted so badly to gain more confidence. So, I started noticing the small achievements and wrote them all down. I set daily goals, and as I collected each day's accomplishments, my confidence grew. Did I eventually get the confident swagger of Oprah? Well, no, that never happened. (Honestly, I'm still waiting to be as confident as Oprah, but who isn't?) But I did gain confidence, and it grew from the ideas I learned from my mom. My brain really was listening, and I started telling it to think higher and dream bigger, because I was ready.

I was teased a lot as a young kid. I hated that feeling, and I promised myself that if I ever saw someone who looked like they were feeling the way I felt in those times, I would extend a helping hand or do my best to help them feel like they were worthy. I learned at a young age the power of compassion. Just listening to someone can make a big difference, and it has helped me to be empathetic to others.

The times when everything seemed to come together, I would feel like I was untouchable or that I was just in such a good rhythm that nothing could knock me off my path. I know what those moments feel like, and I also know now that they don't happen all the time. The times when I felt like I came so close but just not close enough, I never blamed anyone. I learned from my mom that unless I took responsibility for my actions, I wouldn't have the power to fix them. I took a hard look in the mirror and held myself accountable for moments where maybe I could have given more or learned from my mistakes. I also felt that it was important to accept disappointments with grace—yes, those moments may have been disappointing, but they weren't total failures. There were moments where I got to learn more and do better. Being accountable for my mistakes and my successes was a strategy that I took right from my mom's playbook.

As an athlete, you learn that good habits create good results. My mom encouraged me to practice some habits when I was young, like being organized with my time and things and writing down goals. I didn't understand until I was much older how important these habits would be and what an impact they would have on my life.

Learning and practicing qualities like empathy, having a healthy perspective, and showing kindness to others has been so valuable to who I am as a person. When I moved across the country in my twenties, I felt like an adult for the first time in my life. I had the chance to reflect, and

I realized that all of those lessons I'd learned—the way I was mindful of other people, the way I was accountable for my actions, the way I talked to myself—it was all because of my mom.

It wasn't until I was older that I realized the undeniable feeling of thinking that I could do anything was a seed my mom had planted so many years ago. While she had planted those seeds, it took my own personal journey to let them bloom. I didn't just gain these perspectives; they were lessons I had learned from the time I was a child.

Being a parent means being a teacher at the highest level. It's a balance of influencing your child to do better and being their ultimate cheerleader. I will never be able to say thank you enough to my mom. Growing up and becoming an adult is a wild ride. But on this wild ride, I've learned how far being kind to one another and ourselves can really take us. It was when I finally applied all the lessons I learned from my mom that I was able to go out and be my best every day. I learned from my mom that being my best was the mindset of a champion, and my mom taught me to be a champion, on and off the ice. I'm sure there were times when my mom wasn't certain if what she was doing was the right thing, but I always looked to her and admired how she was never afraid to take risks. I take that Kelly Rippon mentality into everything I do.

I am so proud of the book my mom has written, and I'm so excited for you to read it. There is no one in the world who I admire more than my mom. She has always been my hero, and I'm sure that by the time you finish this book, she will be yours too.

Adam

Understanding Influence

Imagine having the power to effect change without forcing it to happen—possessing an invisible yet persuasive presence that can sway the people and things around us in a positive way. Guess what? We all have this power. It's called influence.

Influence is not meant to be intimidating or demanding. It isn't manipulative or magical. Influence is certainly powerful, but it's also casual and inviting.

Long-standing leaders who intentionally use influence are successful because they're patient. They understand that their influence needs to gradually grow in power over time to make a deep impression.

Superinfluencers on social media take this understanding a step further by steadily promoting the usefulness of a product or an idea over time. This builds trust with and buy-in from their audiences. These influencers gain greater credibility if they are using the product themselves.

By regularly demonstrating the product or idea, the influencer makes their endorsement believable and becomes more readily accepted by their audiences. Eventually, it becomes a routine practice.

This book addresses the influencer with the most power to effect change in today's world: the parent. A parent has the greatest opportunity to be the most significant influence in their child's life. The voice of a credible parent surpasses the pull of social media or enticing trends. As parents build their credibility, they promote a trustful atmosphere where children feel safe and develop solid self-esteem. When a child's confidence climbs, their success is inevitable. Sounds easy, but being a parent today is complicated.

Too often, parents are offered advice that is untested by the person giving it, frequently requiring a large support system and a larger bank account to execute it. These overpromised ideas often lead parents to failure. They end up feeling more stressed and less confident in their abilities.

What if I told you that good parenting can develop into great leadership? That using the influential behaviors found in solid leadership to empower your kids is free and only requires you, the parent, to set it into action? What if I also told you that consistently practicing these influences will inspire you and, over time, will improve everything around you?

In the chapters that follow, I will break down the strategies for creating these empowering influences, which will grow a parent's confidence to be a more positive influence and ease some of the complexity in parenting. No doubt, being an effective parent requires a dynamic skill set, because parenting is more than being a caregiver. It's about leading and inspiring others to have an optimistic outlook. It's about using the right words and developing the best habits. It's about having the grace to deliver bad news and the empathy to compassionately explain it. Parenting isn't a uniform that you put on and take off. When we *Parent Up,* we practice the uplifting ideology that includes all of the best influences. It helps us see the upside of life and focus on the positive aspects in the experiences we encounter. When practiced over time, as you will discover in this book, amazing things of Olympic-sized proportions can happen.

A Medal of Influence

I had always thought I understood the power of influence on a basic level, but at the 2018 Winter Olympics in Pyeongchang, South Korea, I realized how deep an impact an influencer could have. My oldest son, Adam, was a member of the United States' bronze medal–winning figure skating team. A few nights before closing ceremonies, the athletes, judges, medical staff, and families gathered in the USA House, about an hour's drive from the Coastal Olympic Village, to celebrate their success. The weather was bitterly cold, and there was a steady snowfall as our bus carefully made its way around the winding roads to the mountain venue.

During the ride, I discovered an Olympic tradition that most people don't know about. All of the U.S. Olympic medalists get a second medal, known as the Order of Ikkos. This medallion is threaded on a long ribbon and mirrors the gold, silver, or bronze composition of the Olympian's medal. It has all of the Olympic markings, but the medal is created from a different mold and embossed with a lit Olympic torch raised by a person with two hands and supported by another individual with one hand. You don't see the faces of the people lifting the torch. They symbolize the *unseen* support behind the athlete. The medal is named after Ikkos of Tarentum, who was the first Olympic coach in ancient Greece. This medallion is presented to the medalists, who then give it to the person who they feel has been the most influential in their journey toward achieving their Olympic prize. Understandably, most athletes have historically awarded the medallion to their coach or trainer. I was excited to find out that we were gathering for more than just a party and looked forward to the special event.

I thought about this Order of Ikkos and wondered why I had never heard of it before. I wondered if Nathan Chen, Adam's training mate, would give his honor to their coach, Rafael Arutyunyan. If he did, Adam might consider giving his Ikkos tribute to his secondary coach, Derrick Delmore. Derrick was like a big brother to him. I also thought Adam may give it to his trainer, Brandon Siakel, who had been instrumental in Adam's recovery from breaking his foot just a year earlier. Regardless of whom Adam selected, I looked forward to listening to the appreciative speeches from the athletes that night.

As we journeyed up the winding, snow-covered roads to the Mountain Cluster venue for this ceremony, it concerned me to see abandoned cars that had slid off the road, some of which were turned completely around. Somehow, we arrived unscathed. We all clapped as we pulled into the parking lot and high-fived the driver as we exited the bus. We walked a short distance to the USA House, and once inside, I looked around in search of Adam, who had been on a separate bus with people coming from the athletes' village. He was sitting with the other athletes and waved to me as I entered.

The presentation started a few minutes later. This kind of ceremony fosters a heightened sense of community among elite athletes and the people who support them. Judges, coaches, parents, and team members sat close together on couches or stood leaning on each other. We were all scrambling for tissues as we listened to the heartwarming tributes shared by the athletes. I sat next to American ice dancer Madison Chock. This was her second Olympics, so I relied on her as my event guide, and she was kind enough to answer my questions. We sat close to the front of the room and cried and supported each other as Maia and Alex Shibutani spoke so eloquently about the tremendous appreciation they felt for the influence their coaches had on their careers. We wiped our tears as they each awarded the medallions to their coaches.

Adam was the last to speak. My eyes began to tear up when his name was announced. I grabbed a tissue and looked up toward him standing confidently in front of the jam-packed room. Behind him were three large media screens, displaying the U.S. Figure Skating logo in the center with the U.S. Olympic team logo on either side. He looked so calm, so comfortable in front of the crowd. I was so impressed with how he was managing the stress of the past few weeks. His competitive events were in the first week of the Games, and once they were over, his days were filled with morning-to-night interviews and media commitments. The pace he was keeping and the demands on his time didn't show as he relaxedly took the microphone and set the tone with a joke. The entire room laughed and leaned in as he continued to speak. As the oldest member of the figure skating team, Adam had an eighteen-year relationship with skating that went bone deep. He brought all of us along on the emotional ride of his personal Olympic quest. He recognized his coaches, his trainers, the federation, his sponsors, and fans and friends that helped him along the way. Then came the moment that I can best describe as immense pride colliding with utter disbelief.

Adam reached out his arms, medal in hand, and said, "Even with the support from all the people who helped me along the way, none of this would have been possible without my mom. She always believed in me and has been the biggest influence in my life. No matter what, she always encouraged me to believe in myself like she did. She always found a way to support my skating, even after my parents divorced. She told me I was a champion since I was a little kid. At first, I thought being a champion was about winning medals. But as I grew older, I learned that being a champion is a mindset. I want to honor my mother with the Order of Ikkos for always believing in me and having such a great influence in my life."

I was shocked. I could feel the tears rushing down my face as Madison pulled me to my feet. She hugged me and pushed me toward the center-stage area, where Adam was standing. I had my hand cupped over my mouth, speechless, as he placed the medal over my head. We hugged, and he said jokingly into the microphone, "Mom, there may be a catch. They told me that a parent has never received this before. Don't worry, you get to keep it, but they're going to make you take the coach's exam!" The room roared with laughter, and I was finally able to exhale and appreciate the moment.

After the ceremony ended, we all stood around the room hugging each other and chatting, and fellow Olympic parents and some of the officials shared how impressed they were with Adam's remarks. The U.S. Figure Skating performance director confirmed that I was the first parent who wasn't also a coach to be honored at the Olympics with this award. They asked how I felt about being credited as Adam's biggest influence. I smiled, shrugged my shoulders, and said nothing. I wasn't being gracious or modest. I was confused and struggling to connect the reality of the last eighteen years supporting Adam the best I could with the present moment and the great honor that he had bestowed upon me. I learned in those few minutes that when you are thrust into the deep end of the public-scrutiny pool, people expect you to swim. I watched Adam answer questions so effortlessly and engage enthusiastically with interviewers and fans. He was swimming. I was trying not to drown.

The Power of Prophecy

Following the Olympics, Adam went on a media tour, where he talked about the influences he experienced in his childhood, including my parenting philosophy. He shared stories of the unusual ways he was held accountable as a kid and how living those lessons had served as a great influence in building positive habits and helping shape his character. Out of the many stories he shared, there was one in particular that seemed to resonate with everyone who heard it, that prompted questions and discussions, and that turned heads my way: the story of a prophecy I wrote for our family on our back porch.

It happened in 2004. I was newly divorced with six children aged three, five, seven, ten, twelve, and fourteen years. I spent the first few weeks after my ex-husband moved out sorting and assembling the disheveled contents of the house. I realized that the divorce had shuffled more than our stuff; it had also jumbled our family focus. I was determined to get us back on track and reunite our family.

I did my best to create an inspiring environment and hung up positive messages, such as "Dream Big" or "Mistakes Lead to Discoveries," in plain sight for encouragement. With each passing day, we grew more organized as a family team. As my confidence increased, I gradually learned to stop second-guessing myself. One momentous Saturday, I woke up with a new sense of determination. I felt filled with answers instead of questions. I made a conscious decision that morning to move from being the *object* to the *subject* of my life's sentence. Going forward, I would do my best to accept what came of the day and use it to my advantage instead of being flooded with frustration. I looked around our home and felt proud of how much we had accomplished during the three months since my divorce. I felt grateful. Gratitude can push you into a mindset that is transformative and life-changing. It gives you a wider view. It helped me see beyond my focus on us as a family unit. I began to understand that it was intentionally honoring our independent interests that was actually fueling our transformation. It was those special qualities that were uniquely inspiring to each of us. I wanted to remind us of that and create a home within a home for each of my children and me.

I realized that the notes of inspiration hung throughout the house were encouraging, but they were general in nature. I knew the messages needed to have more detail, so everyone would feel their own individual significance. I wanted the kids to feel like this was a beginning, not an ending. I didn't realize that what I was about to do would change my life, and my children's lives, forever.

I understood the *why* behind my idea. The *what* and *where* came to me as I sat in my family room that momentous Saturday and looked out the glass French doors to the deck outside. I remember thinking that it was a perfect spot. It was in plain sight. The deck railing offered more than twenty feet of white canvas. It wrapped around the outside of the house like a wooden embrace. I wanted to write a message about each of us that was specific enough to suggest a distinct frame but general enough to offer choice without expectation. The idea also had to be big enough to be relevant for a lifetime. The messages had to be journey-oriented, not destination-driven. As I thought of each of my children and reflected on their individual sparks of brilliance, the words came easily to me.

My life's sentence would no longer be a question. It was a declarative statement, and I wanted to make it black-and-white for my children and the universe we lived in to see. I filed through a box of art supplies and picked up a fat Sharpie Magnum permanent marker. It felt heavy. My hand shook as I marked the pristine banister with indelible black paint. I paused after writing the words, then sat back and read them aloud:

In this home lives Adam, a champion; Tyler, a creator; Brady, a genius; Jordan, a master teacher; Dagny, a leader; Sawyer, a multitude of joy; and Kelly, who is blessed with abundance.

The day I painted the influential porch prophecy wasn't the day the text was written—it was the day it was published. There's a difference. The message I wrote wasn't an arbitrary prediction. It was more of a proclamation of believable testimony. Adam and his brothers and sisters started writing their own stories long before I wrote anything on the porch.

I wrote big-picture descriptors of the kids to let each of them fill in the details as they grew. I assigned the moniker *champion* to Adam because he was resilient, disciplined, and willing to improve his weaknesses instead of ignoring them. Those qualities are what make a champion. I didn't write "Adam, Olympic medalist." That's a goal or prediction. Having qualities of a champion, he could have excelled at many things.

The message I wrote documented who I believed the children were already, not who I hoped for them to be one day.

All my children demonstrated the qualities of each of the designations I assigned them. I wasn't complimenting them; I was offering an authentic acknowledgment of their strongest qualities. That is powerful. It invites confidence. If someone you respect says in a matter-of-fact way that you are a genius or a leader, you are more likely to believe it. You begin to act like a genius or a leader more intentionally. You don't feel pressured to create something to meet someone's expectation. You feel more like you're continuing something that *is* already.

There wasn't a ceremonial reveal or conversation about the porch writing. Because I was a philosophy teacher, my kids understood that I addressed life as a potential 24/7 self-development seminar. It wasn't

Did my kids always listen and follow my directions exactly? No, but most often they made good choices. Words should invite us to think and influence us to make our own best decisions. Like sitting around a conference table in any headquarters, our dinnertime discussions included updates on what Adam and I had missed, grievances about what the younger kids felt was unfair, and general remarks about the difficulties of managing others from the older boys. I loved these dinners almost as much as I loved being their CEO. Having something positive to look forward to, like our nightly dinner meetings, made the long drive easier.

Words Have Meaning

There were many reasons why having dinner as a family every night was so important to me. But the main one was that I knew Adam would eventually have to move to New Jersey to increase his training regimen. I knew that *all* of the kids would eventually move somewhere. The seven of us around the table for a meal was temporary, so I was determined to make the most of it. Instead of a formal prayer to start the meal, we would each mention something we were grateful for. Eyes would roll when one of them would give a lame standby answer like "I'm thankful for our food," or "I'm thankful for Mom." We usually offered them a do-over. I would reinforce the idea that words are important, and we shouldn't use them as placeholders for what we mean to say or what we really want to say. "I'm thankful for our food" was a placeholder.

We repeated this schedule five days a week for several months. By late April, Craig, the skating director at the Ice House in Hackensack, approached me and asked how I was keeping such a crazy pace. What was my secret? I told him that I didn't have a secret. I made a conscious effort to tell myself before the start of every day that it was temporary. "It's temporary" was the deliberate self-talk that I repeated. The notion that this complex and often frustrating schedule could be a permanent plan would be too overwhelming even for the most organized person. I engaged in it one day at a time, and I reminded myself that it was a temporary fix until we settled on a workable solution. I asked myself to hold on until a more long-term plan was revealed. With this in mind, I felt like a winner at the close of each day instead of feeling fearful of and exhausted by what was potentially ahead of me. I quieted my negative-talking, inner doom boss with the phrase, "It's temporary."

A person can do or endure almost anything with the mindset that it's temporary. Think about a woman in labor. At some point, most new moms-to-be ask the nurse how much longer her labor will last. The nurse usually replies, "You're almost there. That baby will be in your arms tonight." The nurse's message is "it's temporary," and the pain or discomfort will be over soon.

Imagine if instead the nurse said, "Who knows how much longer? Your labor could last forever." Any mother would be completely over-whelmed hearing the second response. It's about telling ourselves the best words to develop a mindset that envisions the light at the end of the tunnel. "It's temporary, Kelly." In other words, I knew it was doable. Our reality is greatly influenced by the words we tell ourselves.

**We can lessen stress, contain worry,
and save ourselves from overreaction by
communicating the right words.**

A month later, we saw the light at the end of our weekly thirteen-hundred-mile tunnel. Our temporary fix ended, and a workable solution was found when Adam moved into an apartment in Hackensack a few blocks from the rink in late May.

Dictionary Words Define Facts

There is also a light at the end of the kindergarten tunnel! It's highlighted by a class graduation in the school gym, where families gather with cameras in hand to document the occasion. I was excited and a little sad that it was my *last* kindergarten graduation. Sawyer was excited and anxious to find out what award he would earn. The kindergarten graduation awards were as big as the Oscars in my town. Each of the twenty students were given a "best at" award. The school added a Mr. or Ms. before the title to make it official, and the kids loved it. Parents were nervous, wondering who would win Mr. Kindness, Ms. Helpful, or Mr./Ms. Athlete. I clapped with the other parents as Mr. Politeness and Ms. Best Manners received their awards. *What a wonderful program*, I thought. Then the big reveal came as Sawyer's teacher announced over the public-address system, "Sawyer Rippon, class of 2007, may you forever be known as *Mr. Agreeable!*"

What? I was confused. I turned to my son Brady, sitting next to me, and asked, "Did his teacher just name him Mr. Preamble?"

What is that? I thought.

"No, Mom, she said Mr. Agreeable," Brady answered, trying not to laugh. His mouthful of wire braces made it difficult for him to contain his reaction.

I forcefully nodded my head like I was acknowledging a sudden flash of total clarity, and I tried my best to keep a neutral resting face. But I was confused. The entire year, the teacher had told me how kind Sawyer was, how engaged and helpful. But agreeable? What kind of title was that? I could see that Sawyer was thrilled, but he probably didn't understand what *agreeable* meant. Better stated, he had no idea what I understood agreeable to mean. To me, it screamed, "Follower without goals." To my older children, it clearly meant the same. My controlled reaction wasn't fooling Brady. When we got home later that day, Brady pulled aside his older brother Tyler, who had missed the ceremony, and told him about it.

"Sawyer won Mr. Doormat today at his kindergarten graduation. You know, the one who's most likely to get walked all over."

Brady and Tyler laughed but kept their amusement out of Sawyer's earshot. The kindergarten graduate was busy with his crumbled, hand-crafted coffee filter glued atop a blue grosgrain ribbon, which served as his kindergarten gold medal. I looked at Sawyer's face, beaming with pride. I smiled along, and we celebrated. Later that night after the kids went to bed, I relied on the objectivity of my dictionary. It's important that we sanction words with the proper context, and dictionaries aren't emotional. They offer the universally appreciated meaning of words. I opened my favorite book and found:

AGREEABLE

/əˈgrēəb(ə)l/ *adjective* friendly, pleasant, delightful

Interesting. The dictionary didn't list *doormat* as a possible synonym. It was my prejudice that convinced me to think it meant something other than delightful.

I vowed to remember that a quality life is about feelings based on facts and to trust the dictionary. It is without bias. It is absent of emotions or tone. I found my notebook and journaled this experience. I wrote how my bias prevented me from a fist-pump moment at Sawyer's ceremony. I wrote down experiences that I did not want to repeat. Weeks or months after an event had passed, reviewing the notes that I'd penned grew my awareness. I could see the evidence that words were influencing me.

Written Words Are Powerful

Written words have additional power. When ideas are trapped on paper, they no longer randomly float in and out of our thoughts, shapeless and unclaimed. A written word is stable and provides the reader access to the idea as an observer. Understanding the dynamic nature of words and their power can provide us the encouragement and guidance we need during challenging transitions. Our words hold enormous influence in parenting and leadership.

> **There's something about the dynamic sensory action of reading, discerning, comprehending, sanctioning, and intentionally storing written information.**

There's a reason why we feel the urge to trust a fortune cookie or a newspaper horoscope more than a spoken remark from a reliable friend. We can see written words. We can touch them. When words offer us more sensory exposure, they suggest to us greater credibility and invite us to feel a stronger sense of connection.

When we write down or read written words, something special

happens in our brains. The information is internally and externally stored. Internally, when our brains file information, they analyze it. Neuroscientists call this storage the encoding phase. It's the encoding process that converts the static information into dynamic action. The external message serves as a tangible instruction and activates the encoding process.

At the U.S. Figure Skating Championships in 2008, Adam won the gold medal in the junior men's division. To some, his rise to the top of the ranks seemed meteoric, but I knew that wasn't true. There was no disputing that the training change he'd made to an Olympic-level coach in New Jersey had brought his skills to a noticeably new level. People we once watched on TV were now creating his programs, offering advice, and training alongside him.

Transitioning to the elite level of any sport is a big change, not just financially but also in terms of the expectations of people around the athlete, like coaches and sponsors and even fans. When an athlete moves up the ranks in a subjectively judged sport, the climb can be bumpy, and each mercurial bump reminds the athlete of the fickleness of the sport. Perhaps that's why victories in figure skating are celebrated with separate and elaborate award rituals, complete with past champions bestowing their respected endorsement upon the new "best thing." After his championship-winning performance in 2008, Adam was inundated with television interviews, photo shoots, and federation commitments. I only got to see him for a few minutes after the competition. He saw me waving in the stands after they announced his score, and afterward he walked to where I was sitting. I leaned down under the railing to give him a hug, and he told me that he had to stay at the arena for interviews and would meet me later after the awards ceremony. He suggested that I go back to the hotel and have dinner without him. I made my way out of the rink and grabbed a shuttle back to the hotel.

When I returned to the arena a few hours later, I noticed congratulatory messages on the TV monitors with the words *USFS Junior Men's Champion Adam Rippon*. I struggled to actually believe it. To accept the veracity of written information, you must be in the present moment. That day I wasn't fully there in the present; I was actually straddling it. I had one foot in the past, highlighted by my divorce four years earlier, and one foot in the frighteningly exciting future.

Just before the junior men's medal ceremony, a volunteer approached me on the concourse and asked if I was Adam's mother. I said I was. She told me that a woman had given her a package to deliver to me before the awards ceremony. She handed me a puffy manila envelope. I took it and thanked her. I cut it open, slipped my hand into the envelope, and retrieved a handwritten note:

Dear Kelly,

I was told you're a single mom, and I wanted to give you this flag in appreciation of the sacrifices you are making for your son. When we met Adam, he told us how grateful he was for all that you do for him, and I wanted to make sure he had a ceremony flag for his victory laps! I know that one day he will represent our country at the Olympic Games, and I hope that you will bring this flag with you.

—Your biggest fan!

I looked inside the padded envelope and saw an American flag folded the proper way, the way I learned as a young Girl Scout. I put the note in a side pocket of my wallet, rolled the envelope up, and slid it into my purse. I politely pushed my way through the crowd and got as close to the ice as I could to watch the awards ceremony. After Adam received his medal, he skated toward the boards where I was standing. I handed him the flag and told him that it was given to me by someone he'd met earlier, but I didn't know who they were. He gave me a big hug and draped the large flag around his shoulders like a superhero cape. He skated his victory lap at nationals with immense pride. Hundreds of cameras flashed from multiple directions, and I was surprised by how much attention he was given. I was even more surprised by how comfortably he was managing it all. I started to notice things. The fog was lifting, and I began to stand straighter in the present moment as I repeated the words silently: *Wake up. This is really happening.*

Words can orient us. I smiled as I saw him skate laps around the rink, greeting fans at the boards. Afraid that the flag would inadvertently get misplaced, I tried my best to follow Adam's movement and keep my eyes on it. I carefully collected the flag after the medal ceremony. Keeping it safe suddenly felt like an overwhelming responsibility. I folded it up, slid it into the envelope, and put it back in my purse.

Sanctioned Words Confirm a Plan

When I was alone later that night, I read the note again. It was the first time that I'd seen the words *Olympic Games* and *Adam* in the same sentence. There's a superstition in elite sports: athletes and families don't talk about "going to the Olympics." It just isn't done. People outside of the sport would often ask, "Is Adam training for the Olympics?" The most frequent response I would give started with a confused look, as if to suggest that I had never heard of the Olympics. That normally would be followed by my reply, "Oh my, we don't think about that. He just loves to skate."

I came to find that this is the standard response repeated by every parent I've ever encountered at the elite level.

Sometimes, in a moment of fear, thoughts about the Olympics would float into my consciousness uninvited. I would get noticeably uncomfortable and try to dismiss them. But when I read the note about Adam going to the Olympics, it was different. Reading words that someone else had written seemed to permit the leap from possible to more probable. Reading written words independent of my hand felt safe. I wasn't uncomfortable. For the first time, I entertained thoughts of what it might be like to watch Adam enter a stadium for the opening ceremonies at the Olympics or for me to lead a chorus of fans cheering "U-S-A" at the top of my lungs from the stands, staring down at the Olympic rings. It was fun to daydream. I kept the note and my sporadic Olympic daydreams private, but I brought that flag to every international competition I attended. I proudly waved it from the stands in Bulgaria, Russia, China, Japan, France, Italy, Canada, and Finland, as well as every international competition hosted in the United States. When warranted, I happily handed it over to Adam for his victory laps. On occasion I nervously loaned it to his teammates or to a photographer for on-ice photos. I was always mindful of the flag's whereabouts and felt a duty to keep it secure from harm.

Written Words Are Evidence

The gift I received at nationals in 2008 was much more than a flag with a note. It was evidence. That's what written words are: evidence. When I accepted the flag that day, I curiously read the note, discerned its relevance, comprehended its meaning, sanctioned its truth, and intentionally stored this new information: my son would represent our country at the Olympic Games. I had no idea at the time that this journey would weave and wind through the next three Olympic cycles, four more world-level coaches, five new training cities, and ten years of grueling physical punishment. But, like all good evidence, it was eventually validated.

In 2018 Adam was named to the U.S. Figure Skating Olympic team. When I proudly made the trip to Pyeongchang for the Games, I brought the flag that had invited daydreams, the flag that had served as my trusted companion at international competitions, the flag that I had protected for ten years. The words in the message actualized. I attended every practice in South Korea shrouded in patriotism. There's a lot of downtime at skating competitions, and the Olympics were no exception. The flag became my security blanket. I found myself clutching it to steady my nerves, twisting it to occupy my restless hands, and using its calming presence to smother the fears that would pop into my head.

The flag was popular in the stands in Pyeongchang, and many people asked to borrow it for pictures. I wasn't as nervous about it being passed around at the Olympics. There was a peace about it being touched by so many people. I understood the awesomeness of this cloth and its journey. It seemed a blink ago since I had opened the taped manila envelope at nationals in 2008 and read the note that forecasted this day. Memories rushed into my thoughts of the young fans in Bulgaria who started Adam's first international fan club when he won his first World Junior Championship in March 2008. Images of the enormous crowds of Japanese fans giving him a rock-star welcome came to mind. Grand Prix and world competition memories in France, China, Canada, Russia, and Italy flooded my brain. Tears filled my eyes as these memories came into focus. Now, seeing the flag, my faithful companion, being passed about in the stands, it hit me as I said to myself, *Wake up. This is really happening. You're sitting in the arena at the Olympics.*

I stopped thinking, stopped talking, took a breath, smiled, and began to take it all in. I sat alongside Adam's sister Dagny, his brother Brady, and Dallas, who is Adam's coach's mother. We rose to our feet and chanted "U-S-A" while gazing at the Olympic rings. We held our Stars and Stripes high as the words "representing the United States, Adam Rippon" were announced, resounding through the arena.

Unknowingly, every time I touched that flag over the ten years leading up to that exhilarating moment at the Olympics, I was mentally preparing and subtly formulating a plan. The flag was a tactile trigger that stimulated my brain to recall that "knowing" message, "Adam will represent our country at the Olympic Games." Once recalled, it was awakened in my consciousness as fact, and I unwittingly complied with all opportunities that pulled me in that direction. Written words have a special force. They have an invisible force that causes visible action.

The written note I received from a woman I never met made a huge impact on my life. It influenced the way I thought. I unknowingly was analyzing it, processing it, and synthesizing it into action. I carried it with me for ten years. It was externally stored. Reading what someone else was thinking, and what I was only secretly dreaming about, empowered me. It helped me believe that my far-out idea was possible. The woman who sent me that note never knew how deeply it affected me. That is the beauty of planting seeds of influence with words. It's selfless. You get high from the kind act of planting the idea, and it's so satisfying to use that power selflessly. It isn't necessary to wait and watch. You trust. The woman who attached a handwritten note to the gift she gave me offered the influence of words. Her words were cool and casual. She requested that I bring the flag as if she had the confidence that it would happen. That assuredness shifted me. It raised me to a new level of confidence, all from her influence of words.

Acknowledge with Words

Once words are sanctioned, when we agree that they are likely to be true, they have incredible staying power. I've encountered middle-aged adults who still struggle with the negative thoughts from a nickname or a label they were given as a child. Teasing can be lighthearted, but in a vulnerable mindset, a young mind (or not-so-young mind) may accept a destructive idea as the evidence that prompts them to quit, lose motivation, or sabotage themselves. Be mindful of the incredible power of words.

Words can inspire. In the workplace, I advise managers to add specifics to their favorable reviews. Phrases like "good job" and "productive outcome" carry little weight. Adding details creates greater impact: "You are a superior listener, and because of this quality, you have saved this company from losing the Smith account, one of our biggest clients." The latter phrase is weighted with details. It's personal and evidence-based. This practice of honestly acknowledging your kids' best behaviors promotes their confidence and charges their motivation. Detailed acknowledgments aren't empty or generalized compliments. Instead of saying, "You're nice" after seeing your child share or help someone, give more detail for their brain to store. Consider saying on the way home, "I saw you share your snack with Erin today; that was generous of you. The world is a better place because of generous people." It observes the action and objectively defines the value.

Recognizing the best in our kids helps them to be better.

Write the Right Words

Science supports the adage that you're more likely to reach your goals if you write them down. Research suggests that writing down goals makes them 1.2 to 1.4 times more likely to happen. That's 20 to 40 percent more probable! I remember watching an interview with Bob Bowman, the longtime coach of Michael Phelps, the most decorated Olympic athlete. He said that writing down goals helps create a roadmap for your brain. He shared that Michael had a faithful habit of writing down his goals and keeping them private near his bedside. Michael would then read them to help him get motivated and remind him why he was doing what he was doing.

I think we've all been guilty of entering a store without a shopping list and exiting the store with more than we planned but without what we intended to buy in the first place. That is what it is like to live each day without a written goal. Sometimes you remember your intentions;

sometimes you get distracted. With a note in hand, our brain honors those words like a checklist. The words we write are directions. It is helpful to begin the habit of writing lists and setting goals early with our kids. Journals are for parents too! Keep a journal or notebook, and schedule time in the morning or at night to write your goals down. I have long-term goals, but I create a daily goal as well.

We Become Our Words

We can read the statistics about popular trends and the benefits of developing positive habits. But it is always comforting to see it with our own eyes, especially when it's unexpected. I have always given my kids privacy regarding their phones, emails, journals, and friend groups. One day, long before laptops and iPads, I needed to use the family computer that was stationed in the kitchen. I was locked out, and the error message said that user AdamR needed to sign back into their email to unlock the browser. I tried various ways to solve it, but I couldn't. As a last resort, I called the kids' school and asked for Adam to call me. A few minutes later, Adam called me from the school office. I explained what happened and asked if he could share his password with me because I needed to use the computer. He anxiously offered a few ideas to troubleshoot the problem other than giving up his password. I explained that I didn't have success with any of them, and the easiest way to fix it was to simply unlock his email and close it. I could hear the reluctance in his voice.

He eventually mumbled, "I am a winner number one."

It confused me, and I asked him to repeat it.

"Mom," he protested as his voice grew more uncomfortable. "I am a winner number one."

"That's your password?" I excitedly asked.

"Yes," he responded. "It's a capital *I* and a capital *W* with the number sign and the numeral one."

"Got it!" I exclaimed. I told him that it was a fantastic password and that he really was a winner. I also told him that he could change his password once he got home, but I thought it was important to keep writing that he was a winner, because it was a great idea.

Accidentally finding out Adam's password helped me gain confidence in making the decision that he was ready for homeschooling the next year and that skating was more than a hobby. It had crossed into a full-fledged passion. His words revealed this to me.

I was lucky enough to get a peek into Adam's self-talk, and it revealed that he believed in himself in the private moments without the encouragement of others.

IamaWinner#1 isn't a word per se, but it was a meaningful and powerful word tool that influenced a little boy to believe that he deserved to engage in a life beyond his wildest dreams. Last I checked, he was doing just that.

I tried to remain calm and hide my tears. There was a long, painful silence.

About a minute passed, then Adam said, "Mom, it's going to be okay. The universe isn't cruel. This isn't a loss—it's a bigger opportunity. I'm going to give it a purpose and make this my story."

In my mind, in that moment, he won the Olympics.

The ability to transform loss into love is a powerful skill. It changes a setback into an opportunity and shows mastery of perspective.

This experience offered me the evidence that when we influence others, we are influenced ourselves. After his declaration that this was his story, all my doubt melted away. I was positive that he would recover and reach his goal of representing the United States at the Olympics. And he did.

CHAPTER 4

The Influence of Confidence

CON·FI·DENCE

/ˈkänfədəns/

noun

feeling of self-assurance arising from one's appreciation of one's own abilities or qualities

Synonyms: trust, belief, conviction, reliance

Antonyms: distrust, skepticism

A big challenge parents with multiple children face is creating an environment where everyone feels equally valued. Feeling slighted invites thoughts that we aren't enough, which sparks jealousy. Jealousy appears when a person believes that someone else is taking or getting what they want or deserve. Jealousy wears down confidence. It can distort our thinking and convince us to believe the worst about ourselves or the situation. This "less than" feeling is destructive, not just to the person experiencing it but also to those around the affected person. A parent's goal is to encourage a healthy competitive spirit without jealousy or resentment and to raise kids who don't feel slighted. When our confidence grows, it's easier to accept the idea that there's enough success for everyone. We develop confidence by connecting to moments of satisfaction that are earned, not gifted or got by chance.

Sit in Confidence

One elephant in the room after a divorce often comes in the form of a chair. A chair? Yes, that sanctified kitchen chair that was at the opposite head of the table. In our post-divorce home, it loomed empty. It was where their dad sat. It was more like a hole in the kitchen than a chair at the table. At first, I sat there, hoping to make the absence of life less noticeable, and I pulled my youngest's high chair to my spot at the other end. It was the only way the high chair could be pulled to the table, and it gave me time to think of a transition plan.

A few weeks later, I came up with the idea of the Chair of Honor. I explained that whichever child contributed the most to our family, their school, or the world would be honored by sitting in that special seat and would get to start our gratitude chain, my version of the mealtime prayer. The contribution to earn the honor could be a helpful idea, a special service, or a generous act. The kids loved it, and thus the Chair of Honor was born. They did their best to earn that coveted seat each Sunday and hold it for the week. Everyone knew the rules, and everyone knew they had a chance to earn it, because they believed that it was a fair process.

**When the thought that something is unfair
is interrupted before it becomes a belief,
the idea of jealousy can't take root.**

When a person immediately thinks "next time" upon not getting what they want, it nurtures a healthy competitive spirit to emerge. My kids got the chance to practice the habit of being happy for someone else for getting something that they wanted too. When someone "wins" or gets ahead, it doesn't subtract from the efforts we invested. The truth is that there's enough success for everyone. When we feel we have a chance, we are more apt to try, and it's the act of trying that builds confidence.

Kindergarten Confidence

The kindergarten at my children's school invited parents in rotation to visit the class on Fridays throughout the school year and to read a book or share an idea. When it was my turn, I thought it would be fun to be a little different and show the kids Bulgarian rose water that I had brought home from a trip overseas. I planned to let them smell the perfume and tell them stories about Bulgarian customs like Baba Marta Day, a special holiday that celebrates the end of winter and the welcoming of spring. During this holiday, the streets in Bulgaria are lined with red-and-white yarn dolls, bracelets, and tassels. These bicolored symbols, called *martenitsa*, are exchanged to celebrate blessings and the coming of spring. I visited Bulgaria three times for Adam's competitions, two of which took place during the March 1 holiday. My experience of community goodwill impressed me so much that *martenitsa* making and exchanging became a custom in our home.

The teacher loved the idea and excitedly told me that there was a globe in the classroom. She thought it would be fun for the students to locate Bulgaria on the globe. When I arrived in the classroom, I noticed the globe on a high shelf. I turned to the teacher, pointed to the globe, and asked her if she had a step stool for me to retrieve it. Abruptly, a little girl in the first row jumped up and shouted, "I can get it."

Confidence comes more easily when motivation and the probability of a favorable outcome are high. The girl walked over to the shelf and stretched her arms as high as she could, extending them so confidently for something that was clearly out of her reach. She didn't lose confidence; she persevered and started to jump up, trying to get closer. The teacher approached with a step stool, opened it up, climbed up two steps, and grabbed the globe. She handed it to the little girl. The little girl took the globe, and with great excitement, she announced, "I knew I would get it." Then she proudly handed it to me. She was beaming with that winning glow that people get when they complete a goal. There is something about innocence that invites confidence.

Innocence helps a person focus on the goal without putting restrictions on the strategy.

Sadly, if that little girl had been a few years older, she may have resented the teacher for intervening and taking away her control of the method for reaching the goal. She may have even refused to accept the globe from her teacher, because she didn't get it the way she'd planned.

Since most of us are not kindergartners, how can we use innocence to power our confidence?

Innocence Invites Confidence

We deny ourselves successful moments every day because our ego intimidates the spirited, goal-directed kindergartner inside each of us. We set a goal, and instead of driving toward that goal, we get far too caught up in how we are going to get there. Parents often make this mistake with their children and invite frustration by overplanning and being too focused on the details. We get lost in the logistics of a plan and the probability of success, rather than focusing on the bigger picture.

There is something comforting for me about getting on a plane. The only thing I have to worry about is finding my seat. I know that once I find it and buckle up, I am going to end up where I intend to go. I don't have to know how to fly the plane. I just have to put the work in to afford the seat.

Sometimes parents make the mistake of focusing too much on how to fly the plane. When parents try to fly the plane, they end up cheating their kids out of the experience of hands-on learning through troubleshooting and growing critical-thinking skills. These skills are transferable, and they not only produce success but also stimulate the feeling of competence. When our children are young, it is important that they develop big-picture ideas, ideas that are expansive and directed toward big goals. Feeling that we are "good enough" and competent at something is another way that we build confidence.

Parenting Confidence

Most parents are trying their best. It's difficult sometimes, especially when we are bombarded by images of the twenty-first-century ideal parent. We're given the impression that it's our job to raise kids who are popular, athletically coordinated, worthy of the Ivy League, acne-free, television-star-ready, and multilingual. Anything less than that is a parenting failure.

Social pressures can complicate parenting. You don't have to let them. Resisting the pressure to compare our parenting to other families' is one way to start growing some parenting confidence. The more we can focus on the long-term reasons behind our decisions the less we will think narrowly and change course when there's a sudden interruption in our plan. Keep focused on the big picture, and you will have a plan wide enough to see more options. The more options we see, the more likely we are to have the confidence that our parenting goals will be realized. Options arise from big-picture thinking. If our focus is consumed by too many details, we eliminate options, in addition to raising stress, lowering competence, and lessening the probability of realizing goals.

We may think that the little kindergarten girl was beaming with pride because she was able to hand me the globe. The more innocent we are, the purer our confidence is, and it's more likely that our goals are big-picture driven. The girl's goal was bigger than simply getting the globe. That's why it didn't matter if the teacher arbitrarily helped her. Her goal was focused on *being*, not *doing*. That's why she was so elated handing me the globe—because she helped me. Her goal wasn't to be the highest jumper, the best climber, or the strongest student. Her goal was to be a helper, to be helpful. Her smile confirmed her success. Her declaration, "I knew I could do it," recorded the evidence.

If we aren't careful and mindful, we'll lose that big-picture thinking, ultraconfident kindergartner inside us. We become obsessed with the details of what we are *doing* instead of the awesome feeling of what we are *being*. It's the feelings that should be our compass.

Inside Confidence

Remember all those images of parenting and what we're told it should be? With suggestions like that, we can be misled about what success is. Society implies that unless we can see it, touch it, measure it, and have it admired by others, it isn't real success.

As we mature, the results of our *doing* invite public accolades and external impressions, and sometimes our achievements are even awarded a prize. We can get so wrapped up in the public nature of success and in the prizes that certain achievements can bring, because they come with a flood of external energy. But this outside energy can cause us to lose touch with the feeling of success. We are shocked when people who we perceive as successful, people who appear to "have it all," tell us that they feel empty inside. The doing and being states of confidence-building can get conflated. *Doing* is an extrinsic action and can be judged, measured, and compared. *Being* is an intrinsic feeling and is self-regulated. It takes patience to develop that internal strength, but it is at the core of our confidence. The late Carrie Fisher said, "Instant gratification takes too long." Princess Leia was so wise. There isn't a jackpot or lottery windfall in confidence. It takes time. Collecting satisfying experiences builds confidence and perseverance for the long haul.

A Confidence Journey

In April 2001, Stars on Ice came to northeastern Pennsylvania for Scott Hamilton's farewell tour. The producers called practice rinks in each city of the tour and asked the skating directors to find a local boy and send them to the arena to be that city's "young Scott Hamilton" in Scott's tribute number. They were looking for a boy who could stay on his feet and fit into the tour's only designated guest costume, a boy's size small sweater.

Adam could do both. He was on the ice when the producers called our local rink. One of the coaches who answered the phone approached me and asked if he could do it. I had a million questions. She had zero answers. All she said was to be at the arena for a rehearsal the next morning. Adam finished his Wednesday night club session, and we left the rink. I waited until we were in the car to tell him about the show. He wasn't as thrilled as I thought he'd be. It was almost eight o'clock at night and he only had until nine the next morning to wrap his head around it.

After breakfast on Thursday, I gathered Sawyer's things and got ready to take Adam to the arena. Sawyer was only six months old, and I was still nursing him. Since I had no idea how long the rehearsal would be, that meant he needed to come along with us. Not wanting to be late, I shouted up the stairs to Adam and told him we had to get moving. He ran down the stairs, still pushing last-minute items into his bag. We got into the car, and he spent the next thirty-five minutes talking about how excited he was to meet all the national champions who were in the show. I listened and waited for a lull in the conversation to tactfully remind him—without scaring him!—that he was also in the show, and that this was a great opportunity to perform in front of a sold-out crowd of eight thousand people.

When we got to the arena, we were greeted by Jason Dungjen, a former U.S. pairs champion who wore two hats for the production: skater and Stars on Ice production staff. He took us down a long hallway under the concourse. We passed signs with familiar names on the dressing room doors: Jenni Meno and Todd Sand, Renée Roca and Gorsha

Sur, and singles superstars Kristi Yamaguchi, Yuka Sato, Tara Lipinski, Kurt Browning, and Scott Hamilton. I saw Adam's eyes grow wider and his pace quicken with excitement. Jason took us to an office that had the boy's small sweater hanging on a hook behind the door. He said that someone would be back to get Adam in thirty minutes to bring him to the ice and meet the choreographer who would be teaching him the number he was in with Scott.

When Jason left, I nursed Sawyer and did a quick diaper change to prepare for rehearsal. Adam stretched, warmed up, tried on the costume, and rifled through his bag in search of something. I noticed that he pulled out his autograph book.

"Why did you bring an autograph book?" I asked as he held it up over his head after successfully retrieving it from his bag.

"Tara Lipinski, Kristi Yamaguchi, and Scott Hamilton are in the show. I think I'm going to meet them," he said. "I wanted to get their autographs."

"You are in the show too," I told him. "This is a privilege, not fan access."

He looked disappointed. This is when I knew that the big picture needed to be pulled back into his thinking. He was hyperfocused on the detail of meeting his idols instead of the big-picture experience of being in the show.

"Look, Adam, you have a choice. You can leave the book in this room, be a performer, talk skater-to-skater with the cast, and believe that they will be your peers someday. Or, you can bring it with you, be a fan with a backstage pass, and fill up your book with a bunch of names of people you'll have to buy a ticket to see again. If you want to be in the cast someday, then you should act like you belong now. It's your choice."

I was direct and harsh. But harsh or not, my point was to stay big picture and not lose sight of his goals. I reminded him of his options but never told him what to do. Influence doesn't force. Parents can't command confidence to emerge.

He left the autograph book in the dressing room. Adam took the ice, hit his mark in the spotlight, and nailed his single axel.

Confidence Needs Patience

Fast-forward to 2016, when I attended the opening night of the Stars on Ice tour in Hershey, Pennsylvania. I teared up listening as the announcer asked the audience to welcome "U. S. national champion Adam Rippon." I was so proud of the little boy who had left his autograph book in his bag fifteen years earlier. Adam took to the ice yet again, hit his mark in the much bigger spotlight, and nailed his triple axel.

Confidence develops over time. It is such a great feeling when parents get to witness one of their children live in confidence and stay patient long enough to reach their goal. Adam endured what he didn't like in order to do what he loved. He saw the big picture. He understood that patience held the key to confidence. It generally takes dozens of experiences over time to increase to that level of self-assuredness. Sometimes there can be a shifting experience that impacts confidence and advances it to a new level.

A Winner's Confidence

During Adam's novice season, he learned a valuable lesson about the meaning of winning versus being a winner and losing versus being a loser. The first is an action and the latter is a feeling. They aren't the same thing. He was competing at sectionals, the qualifying competition that is the last step before earning a spot at nationals. That season he made a strong impression that he had quality skating skills and a solid triple lutz. However, at sectionals, he made three freak errors. He tripped entering the ice before his program, he caught an edge and fell after his footwork, and he bumped into the boards after losing his footing in crossover transitions. The mistakes were unexpected and unusual. He was embarrassed. He looked at me, shocked, as he exited the ice, before heading to the seclusion of the locker room.

About thirty minutes later, the results were posted on the wall outside the arena, and skaters, coaches, and mothers all clustered to read the results. I scanned the sheet with my heart in my throat, because only the top four got to advance to nationals. At the top of the results sheet, I saw the words "First place: Adam Rippon, Skating Club of New York." I was relieved and a little surprised. I looked around to see if anyone was outraged. They weren't. A fellow skating mom looked at me and said that he'd done a great job. I must have looked puzzled, so she kept talking. She explained that although he got two deductions, the falls were outside the required elements, so they didn't hurt his score as much as if he had fallen on a jump or in the middle of his footwork. I did not study the rules as much as most of the moms did, so I appreciated the clarification. She pointed to an awards ceremony notice. I looked at my watch and realized that it was starting in only fifteen minutes. It was important for the top four finishers to attend, because the local organizing committee took a picture for *Skating* magazine. I thanked her and looked around for Adam.

As I was walking, one of the competitors told me that Adam was packing his stuff in the locker room. I walked back into the nearly empty ice area of the arena toward the boy's locker room. I knocked on the door and heard Adam answer. I cracked the door and asked if he was all right. He said he was alone and that I could come in. I saw that he was wearing jeans and had his coat on. His skates and costume were packed away, and he was holding a large manila envelope. I recognized that envelope. The national competitors each get one, filled with copious amounts of forms that have to be completed and returned. I knew that if he was holding the envelope, he knew the results. I asked him what was wrong—he had won.

He said, "I fell three times. I didn't really win."

I quickly corrected him. "No, you actually won. You got two deductions in the free skate, and, combined with your short program, you won the competition."

He didn't say anything. I told him that they were taking a picture for *Skating* magazine, and he needed to put his costume back on.

He protested, "I don't deserve it. I'm too embarrassed to accept the medal."

Walking toward the door, I stopped, looked back at him, and said, "Adam, I know you feel bad. Remember this moment, because this is what winning feels like sometimes, especially when winning is your only goal. I am sure that the boy who held on to fourth place feels like the luckiest person here, like he won the whole thing. Everyone competing today wanted to win. You have the chance not just to be the winner today but also to feel like a winner and act like a champion." I grabbed the door handle and continued, "You can feel however you want to. Feelings are choices; rules at competitions are not. But you won and with that comes responsibility. I hope you put your costume back on and get to the podium for a picture. The other three boys deserve that respect; so does your coach, and so do you." I left the locker room and returned to the lobby.

Summoning Confidence

A few minutes later, I saw Adam appear in the rink lobby, waiting for the novice men to be called for their awards. He was in his costume. I watched as he proudly stood atop the podium. He earned more than a medal that day. He earned the awareness of what it takes not just to win but also to feel and act like a champion. He went on to earn his first national medal a few months later: a silver in men's novice. It would be the first of many.

> When we condition our spirit to be grateful,
> we condition the spirit of a good sport.

Good sports operate from an attitude that they are enough. This attitude connects us to confidence. Using the influence of confidence activates our inner champion and helps us root honestly for another's success while at the same time staying faithful to our own goals.

Confidence Tells Us What We Want

Adam's arduous journey and his sacrifice of a stable home life gave his brothers and sisters a hard look at what it took to rise as one the best athletes in the world. After he won his first World Junior Championship

in March 2008, we celebrated, and the kids and I were invited to partic-
ipate in a PBS special about young athletes. My other kids participated
in recreational and school sports, and it was around this time that my
youngest daughter, Dagny, started to put more effort into her gymnastics, training at a gym about ten miles away in Scranton. She was very
talented, and her coach, who owned the gym, was honest about its limits
and Dagny's potential. The coach told me that Dagny could go much
farther if she moved to a bigger gym in Allentown, ninety minutes away.
She explained that they had a strong, nationally competitive program
that was worth checking out. I discussed it with Dagny, and ultimately,
she decided not to switch to the more competitive gym.

Asking our kids if they are willing to change their lives for the chance
of moving closer to what they think they want is a complex idea. It would
be easier if they knew all the elements in the big picture of what they
wanted. Was it a "doing" (award-directed) goal, or a "being" (feeling-
directed) goal? She was tearful as she explained her decision. She said
she admired Adam but didn't want his life. She said she loved school
and wanted to go to sleepovers and live at home. She asked me if I
was mad or disappointed. I explained that I wasn't disappointed. I was
proud of her. While she didn't want to disappoint me or her coach, I was
impressed that she was willing to risk it to be true to herself. That was
self-awareness and confidence at its core. She knew what she was willing
to do and what she was willing to do without. She had more than solid
tumbling passes, and she had unusual leadership skills for a ten-year-old.
She loved *doing* gymnastics, but she loved challenging herself even more
and *being* a disciplined risk-taker.

Overconfidence and Underestimation

Dagny volunteered, tried out, and signed up for every available club and activity at school. One day she came home and told me that she was auditioning for the school play. She told me it was *Annie*. I said that her tumbling would be impressive and that I thought she was a shoo-in to be cast as an orphan. She quickly corrected me and said that she wanted to audition for the part of Annie. I didn't know what to say—I didn't know how to tell her that Annie usually has several solo songs to sing. I had never heard her sing or seen her show an interest in singing, and I didn't want her to be disappointed.

I casually asked, "You know that Annie is the lead, and she has several solos, right?"

She quickly replied, "Of course I know."

I was still confused, so I asked her if she wanted some help getting ready for the audition. She responded that she had a plan and was going to prepare by herself.

I was unsure of how to brace her for the likelihood that she would not be singing "the sun will come out tomorrow" in the coming weeks, so I just let it go. The next week, I picked her up after the audition, and she said that the teacher was posting the cast that night, but she thought she got the part.

I grew increasingly worried about her high confidence—she seemed so sure! I was concerned that she was going to be very disappointed. On the drive home, I reminded her about being a good sport and that since she tried out, I expected her to accept any role she was assigned. She told me not to worry, that she knew she'd had a great audition. At the time, I was more concerned about what she was "doing," versus who she was "being."

**Parents are people too. We are human. Sometimes
we can get so consumed by the fear of our kids
facing a huge disappointment that we unknowingly
signal our own lack of confidence in their actions.**

Later that night, she checked the posting online, and—not to her surprise—she was cast as Annie. Six weeks later, I was knocked out by what a beautiful singer and great actress she was. She did have a plan. She was a true leader; she didn't burden me with problems that I didn't have the skills to solve. She gave her best effort, and it brought out the best in her. I was wrong and felt badly about doubting her. By doubting her, not only did I deny her my authentic support, but I also denied myself the joy of her journey. This taught me that when our kids hold more confidence than we do, it's important to give them the space to exceed their limits. I asked her after the show if she was interested in taking singing lessons or auditioning for other shows. She said no. Actually, she said, "Mom, stop." She explained that she didn't audition to start a singing and acting career. She did it to continue pushing herself to try new things. She knew that trying things grows confidence. Dagny used her leadership skills to increase her confidence, and she used her confidence to be a better leader.

It's important that, as parents, we understand that our kids aren't mini versions of ourselves. We should respect the fact that each of our kids is different. They cope differently, they communicate differently, and their desires vary. It is not our job to tell our kids what they should like or who they should be. It's up to us to keep presenting and reminding them of options. Options give us more ways to grow confidence. It's

THE INFLUENCE OF CONFIDENCE

helpful to encourage intrinsic confirmation of success instead of extrinsic rewards. They should build the confidence to know what a good effort *feels* like and strive for that instead of striving for flattery from the compliments that follow success. Compliments aren't evidence of success, and it is evidence that builds confidence.

Confidence Brings Independence

Damaging decisions come from a lack of confidence when the external approval overrides the internal self-belief. It's when we worry too much about what people think. We strive for the outside to look optimal, but the consequence is that we feel empty on the inside. Parents can get so wrapped up in looking like the perfect family to others that they lose sight of how lost their kids really are. Our children's publicly celebrated successes aren't a reflection of our competence as parents. I have found that the highest successes are not the public, *external* kind that kids hold in their hands like a trophy; they are the private, *internal* kind that kids feel in their gut, that spark a passion and drive them to succeed. We as parents need to be a solid, nonjudgmental, unconditional support system for our kids. Undermining a child's competence by negotiating on their behalf, using money or leveraging power to influence outcomes, or comparing them to their classmates or siblings prevents that potential spark of passion from ever becoming a fire in the belly.

Give them time. Give them time to make mistakes, figure it out, and grow confidence. Give them time to feel competent. Give them options to do things and the freedom to feel what they want about those things.

Give them time to feel proud and
invite you to notice.

Parents aren't making their kids' lives easier by covering for their mistakes or bailing them out of trouble. You may temporarily remove the conflict, but you also remove the opportunity for your child to have a fist-pump moment. Fist pumps come from those moments when they can feel that they are indeed enough. Kids who don't earn things don't pump their fists or raise their hands to help others—not because they are incapable but because they are conditioned to believe that they can't do it on their own without outside help. Confidence and its influence are an inside job. You can't buy it, win it, or give it to someone. It is earned.

CHAPTER 5
The Influence of Empathy

EM·PA·THY

/ˈempəTHē/

noun

the ability to understand and share the feelings of

another

Synonyms: awareness, fellowship, affinity

Antonyms: distance, aloofness, standoffishness

Psychologists say that empathy is a work in progress, that it develops over time. It grows as we are exposed to and learn to understand experiences and conditions of people who are different from us. Children begin to understand empathy when they realize that they are an individual person, that other people are separate from them and have different feelings than they do. Empathy helps us identify our feelings and helps us recognize the feelings that are emotionally expressed by of my mouth naturally, without a sense of advocacy, just logical common sense. She paused and said she'd never thought of it like that.

My oldest boy was only seven, but he was old enough to know that he wanted a Barbie, and I didn't want him to feel like he was breaking a rule. I didn't want him to feel that he had to "fake like" something or go along with something that he didn't want to do. I didn't want him to be disloyal to his own desire because of a suggestion by someone else. I didn't want any of them to feel that food and toys were gender restricted.

Loyalty isn't restrictive; it frees us to be ourselves.

Obligated Loyalty

It's vital to be in touch with your core beliefs, in order to figure out what you stand for and in order to set boundaries for those around you. Our loyalty shows us how to demonstrate consistency within those boundaries. Sometimes it's difficult to explain that we have boundaries to people who are offering us a favor or discounting their services for us. We can feel that by setting conditions for accepting those favors, we seem ungrateful, or by questioning someone's judgment, we're being disrespectful.

Our loyalties can shift more easily if we accept that the reason to change them will bring a better outcome than the comfort of the status quo. But conflict can arise when generations collide and out-of-date practices like spanking, forgoing seatbelts, or thinking that it's acceptable to secretly baptize a grandchild in a hospital bathroom are acceptable. (Yes, my mother actually did this.) When differences with family members or people on your support team arise, it's usually because they're holding on to ideas from their past.

People most often get angry for two reasons. The first is feeling attacked for who they are, and the second is feeling an assault on their convictions. Our convictions are the core beliefs that come from our experiences. By presenting ideas that counter people's opinions, we run the risk that they will take things personally and feel attacked. Some of those encounters can be very uncomfortable experiences. Knowing our loyalties and what we stand for can provide guidance on how to move past conflict.

Conflict and Loyalties

The hardest part of having a difficult conversation is starting it.

But steering through it can be an empowering experience. Successfully navigating difficult conversations can clearly define your core beliefs and invite consistency in demonstrating them. Loyalties will only be consistent if aligned with our core values.

I experienced a generational divide that forced me to challenge some of my mother's parenting ideas and convictions. Our concepts of discipline conflicted.

My mother and I had a complicated relationship, but that all changed when she suffered a near-fatal heart attack shortly after my second child, Tyler, was born. After a long hospital stay and triple bypass surgery, the doctors felt that it was best for her to stay with family for a few months during her rehabilitation. My then-husband and I had just moved into our new home, and it made sense that she stay with us, since we had room and I was home all day to help her. After the first week, she was able to take the stairs to have meals with us in the kitchen. Tyler was five months old and Adam was just over two years. Their high energy gave her energy. The more time that passed, the more comfortable my mother felt offering her opinions. I was careful not to push back too much, because I knew from experience that my mother's ideas and my ideas on parenting were not similar, and I didn't want to appear disrespectful. I was able to ignore or talk past most of what I disagreed with, until she corrected Adam with a slap on his hands for getting too close to an electrical outlet.

I reacted quickly and emotionally, saying, "Mom, *we* aren't a hitting family."

She quickly replied, "I didn't hit his hand. I just tapped his hand."

I said, "We aren't a tapping family either."

She moved to walk out of the room, saying defensively, "Fine, next time I'll just let him electrocute himself. I guess everything I ever did was wrong."

I couldn't hear clearly what she said after that, but she continued to talk as she made her way back to her room. Like I said, our relationship was complicated in those days. I knew better than to try to explain my position right away. My mother avoided having a difficult conversation by ignoring me for the rest of the day. That space helped me realize that I had confidence as a mother and was willing to stand my ground. I realized that I had my own convictions, my own loyalties. I also came to realize that we both wanted the same thing. We both wanted Adam to be safe and understand the danger of touching the outlet. It was our beliefs about how to achieve that outcome that differed.

The next morning, Adam ran into Grandma's room to get her to go downstairs for breakfast. I waited at the door holding Tyler, wondering if she was going to speak to me. She walked past me, following Adam to the stairwell without saying a word. Adam squatted to slide down backward on his belly, taking the steps one at a time. This was a slow-moving process, and it afforded me a captive audience. My mother was trapped, with me behind her and Adam in front of her moving at a snail's pace. Uncomfortable conversations are harder to initiate than to navigate. I felt that this was my chance. I went for it.

"Mom, about yesterday. My no-hitting, no-tapping rule has nothing to do with you. I believe that it's the best for my kids, and it's my fault that I didn't explain it earlier, so that you would've known before." I then immediately started baby talking with Tyler, pretending like I didn't expect a response. Once we all got to the bottom of the stairs, she got involved with the kids and never acknowledged what I'd said to her.

Loyalty and Your Integrity

I knew that she understood, but I also knew that I had hurt her pride. I had challenged her convictions. But I had also influenced the way she thought going forward about parental discipline. I learned that most people do the best they can with what they know. That's what my mother did. It's counterproductive to remind anyone what knowledge they lack if you want to share a new idea. I knew by this point in my life that new ideas had to be served buffet style and not force-fed. After this experience,

I learned to communicate with my mom as a confident mother instead of as a wounded daughter. It served both of us going forward.

My mother never hit or tapped any of my kids after that day. My children adored spending time with her, and I loved seeing her transform from a discouraged, pessimistic mother, who I knew had struggled raising her seven kids through abject poverty and abuse, into a confident, trusting grandmother who found and celebrated her value.

Be Loyal to the Truth

In the summer of 1992, she moved to a small apartment only a few miles away. My kids and I saw her nearly every day. She was an integral part of their childhood and over the next two decades became their biggest cheerleader and most loyal fan. She lined her apartment walls with newspaper articles, school programs, and pictures of the kids on corkboards. She got used to only seeing Adam on weekends after a training week. In late 2008 she had mixed feelings when Adam told her that he was moving even farther away to Toronto, limiting his home visits even more. She was born in Toronto, and it gave her great pride to hear him describe the city to her. She loved figure skating and would gather her friends in her apartment building to watch all the competitions on TV.

Her health began to fail in 2013, and she suffered a serious fall with a closed head injury. My brother and sisters and I were able to care for her for the next few years, so that she could stay in her apartment. Sadly, her absentmindedness was a precursor to dementia. It was difficult to watch her forget conversations, misspeak our names, and lose hold of memories. It's scary to watch dementia progress. Mindfulness is less of a challenge in dementia because there's only the now. Dementia has no honest yesterday and can't comprehend a tomorrow. A person with dementia always changes the pieces to fit their picture.

It made me think of how we elevate the value of the personal stuff we hold so closely and how we're so particular about our belongings, until a flood or fire interrupts our life. After an extreme loss, we shift what holds supreme value to the things that meet our most basic needs, like having a place to sleep, food to eat, and people to talk to. Dementia was the fire that turned my mother's personal preferences to ash. Her condition declined to the point that she needed round-the-clock supervision. My siblings and I decided it was safer for her to move to Florida to live with my sister who was a nurse. It was difficult to visit her there. Phone calls and video chats grew awkward. Our names escaped her, and at times she would be confused about time and place or assign us the identities of people she knew from her past. But there were three things that were seared into her memory: she was Canadian, she loved figure skating, and her favorite skater was named Adam.

My sister had a recording of the 2016 U.S. Figure Skating Championships on her iPad. Adam won that year with two stellar performances. My sister would play the recording every morning for my mother to watch after breakfast. She would be thrilled and a little nervous to watch "her Adam" skate and would root for his success with fresh eyes every morning, her short-term memory all but gone. She never said who Adam was, but she knew that she knew him, so she labeled him "her Adam."

"I wonder how he'll do today?" she'd ask, having no memory of watching it the day before. "I hope he wins the whole thing," she'd say nervously.

My sister would go along on the exciting adventure of watching my mother watch "her Adam" win the national championship every day for the first time. I have peace knowing that my mother now has more happy moments than frustrating ones. I learned to be loyal to who she is today instead of who I wished she were a long time ago. I had to be more of a mother to her than a daughter. Parenting evolves only when we can break the cycle of dysfunction rooted in misplaced loyalties. Children who grow up in dysfunction have loyalties fastened to fear. I was fortunate to break away from the limiting ideas about parenting that were handed to me. It was the struggle of breaking free from these misplaced loyalties that helped me grow the strength to stand up for my own beliefs.

Faithful Loyalty

The Catholic elementary school that my kids attended integrated catechism instruction into the curriculum. It included preparation for receiving the sacraments, so they never had to attend Sunday school. I felt that it was more organized having all the kids attend the same school for as long as possible, rather than juggling several schools with different schedules. Their Catholic school had fewer amenities than the public school, but it offered consistent rules and had a much smaller student population. Over my kids' twenty-one-year tenure, I felt like the school was part of my extended family. Granted, sometimes the school acted like a twin sister when we aligned with common ideas, and sometimes it acted like a mean older sister when I felt judged for being divorced, but I knew my kids were safe there.

I disagreed with some of the religious teachings, and I wasn't shy about sharing my opinion with the monsignor. The monsignor was known as a progressive in the church community and a "don't rock the boat" kind of pastor. I sometimes frustrated him with my unconventional thinking, but he supported some of my projects. I pitched the idea of dance movement in the liturgy. The promise that the planned movement I was teaching would still the children's restless feet and hands interested him. He also permitted me to choreograph the children's holiday services. It was a popular feature. He had a candid approach and openly joked that my babies were old enough to ride their bikes to their own baptisms. That wasn't completely true. While it was customary for newborns' baptisms to be scheduled within the first few weeks after their births, my babies were baptized a few months after they were born. I had cesarean deliveries and wanted to be on a decent schedule and in a decent clothing size for their christenings. After all, I knew my mother was secretly baptizing them in the hospital bathroom on her first visit, so I wasn't in a rush. But, overall, I felt that the monsignor was approachable, and I never felt that I was being disloyal to him or the church if I disagreed.

Question Your Loyalties

When Adam was in second grade, I went to the rectory to have a casual conversation with the monsignor about Adam's preparation for his upcoming First Communion. I was uncomfortable with some of the language in the prayer responses. During the Mass at the consecration of the Eucharist, the celebrant holds up the Host and says to the congregation:

> *Behold the Lamb of God, behold him who takes away the sins of the world. Happy are those who are called to his supper.*

The young second-graders were asked to memorize the congregation's response:

> *Lord, I am not worthy to receive you, but only say the word and I shall be healed.*

I had a problem with a seven-year-old memorizing and repeating the line, "I am not worthy." Unworthy? I suggested to the monsignor that it was practicing destructive language to have the young, impressionable communicants affirm that they are unworthy and repeat it multiple times a week when they are in church.

Not surprisingly, he had a problem with my idea of changing the Bible text. He said I was the first parent to have an objection to the response. I found *that* alarming. I told him that I may have been the first person to voice an objection to him firsthand, but I could not possibly be the first person to identify language that worked against a child believing in a loving God.

He looked away like he was thinking and searching his mental files, turned to me, and said, "Actually, you are. No one has ever complained about the Bible verse to me. It surprises me that you found it acceptable for yourself, given that you've been saying it for the past thirty years."

I knew I had a choice to accept his response as a sarcastic mocking of my protest or to accept it as his acknowledgment that I was indeed the first to spot this heinous error in the text. I chose the latter.

"Well, then I consider it an honor," I responded and added, "Thank you for hearing me out."

"I was kidding," he said, laughing.

"Kidding about what?" I asked. "I'm not being picky or a crazy parent; I just can't blindly teach my kids that this language is acceptable. I don't want them feeling like their power comes from something outside of them," I admitted.

"But, it does," he said matter-of-factly. "That's what inviting God in is about."

"Monsignor," I said, as I carefully collected the right words for my reply, "I believe that God is already inside of us. I respect your position. I am not interested in creating a committee or starting a petition. I just want you to know where I am coming from and what I am teaching my own children. I am not rewriting the Bible; I am translating it for my family. My kids are being taught to say, 'Show me that I am worthy,' instead of, 'I know that I am not worthy.' They know it's our *family way*, not a *school way*. There won't be an issue with Adam discussing this with his classmates."

"I can't control what you do in your own house. But the sisters at the school won't be open to discussing this," he said, warning me.

"Adam knows not to offend anyone. He knows the difference," I said, assuring him as he turned toward the rectory door.

He looked back at me and asked, remarking about my physical appearance, "When is your next baby due?"

"Three months," I confirmed. He shook his head with a smile and walked into the rectory. In my naivete, I didn't realize that I was walking away from the rectory that day attempting the impossible. Completely unaware, I was just attempting to be loyal to opposite views.

I was trying my best to stay loyal to the church and my own emerging beliefs simultaneously.

> **Divergent loyalties can't be maintained
> without constant conflict.**

It would take some time for me to figure that out.

Confidence Clarifies Our Loyalties

My emerging confidence as a parent was noticeable, and I think the monsignor knew I was changing. By the time Adam was receiving his First Holy Communion, I was expecting my fifth child. I was engaged in learning as much as I could. I knew my cable television mentor, Dr. T. Berry Brazelton, would be proud of me for speaking up for my convictions and appalled by the corrosive language being taught to impressionable ears. It was important to me that my children had the confidence to know that goodness was already inside them, and they didn't need to have it deposited.

Five more children learned my amended edition of the communion responses. The church changed some of the language in the revised missal in 2011. I was hopeful. Sadly, it was worse and seemed even more inaccessible for kids. Instead of "Happy are those who are called," it was updated to "Blessed are those who are called." But the unworthy line was restructured with even more emphasis and details of unworthiness. The revised response read, "Lord, I am not worthy that you should enter under my roof, but only say the word and my soul shall be healed." By the summer of 2011, all my children had completed their First Communion and were well versed in the Kelly Rippon version of the modern liturgy. I continued to attend church, but my confidence allowed me to start seeing things that I hadn't seen before—things that may have been too fearful for me to accept.

Reevaluating Loyalties

In the spring of 2015, my youngest child, Sawyer, was the last Rippon to graduate from Our Lady of Peace School. In the fall of 2015, my oldest child, Adam, publicly came out as gay. I received many beautiful, heartfelt letters from Catholic priests, mothers, and dozens of gay and lesbian kids, but sadly I also received hate mail from many different people across the country. I kept all of them.

Whether encouraging or damning, each letter offered me an opportunity to reflect on my convictions and how I felt about what I called my extended family. They helped me to reevaluate my loyalties and get in touch with my core beliefs. By 2015, my feeling of worthiness overshadowed any loyalty to catechism. I realized that I was covering for the church's dysfunction, just like my mother covered up for my father's. She'd defend his abuse by saying that, underneath his violent outbursts, he was a good man. I saw myself protecting the church the same way. I'd defend the church and make excuses that it was growing and that, underneath all the conflict, I believed that there was so much good there. I forced myself to reckon with my divergent loyalties, and I knew I couldn't justify the hypocrisy anymore. Hearing the late monsignor's voice in my head haunted me. I wondered why I had never voiced stronger objections when evidence came to light of the rampant child abuse cover-ups in the church. How could I continue to deny the church's attitude toward homosexuality? I had new loyalties. I had evolved. It was time to stop translating what I wanted to hear and just listen.

CHAPTER 9
The Influence of Accountability

AC·COUNT·ABIL·I·TY

/əˌkoun(t)əˈbilədē/

noun

the fact or condition of being responsible; answerable

Synonyms: liability, answerability

Antonyms: unaccountability, irresponsibility,

recklessness

Accountability is a powerful influence. It strengthens character. It's a silent, internal call to do the right thing. Assuming responsibility when things go wrong is uncomfortable. It can cause a swell of unease and confusion. On the bright side, it usually results in us feeling bigger, with a clearer sense of who we are. Holding our kids accountable for their actions may be the strongest influence we can offer them as they mature toward adulthood.

At some point, I declared my third son, Brady, to be my favorite child. I did it for no other reason than to stop the bickering from the other kids, who from time to time would argue about who they thought was my favorite child. Adam and Tyler squabbled over it as did the youngest three, Jordan, Dagny, and Sawyer. I had noticed that Brady didn't seem to care that much about it, so one day, when Adam and Tyler were arguing and asked me in unison, "Mom, who is *really* your favorite?" I appointed Brady. I considered saying that they were all my favorite, but that response, as I knew from multiple times before, didn't put an end to the questions. I felt ready to end the madness and said, "Brady is my favorite. It's a lifetime position, and the rest of you are tied for second." As silly as it sounds, it worked. The subject didn't come up again. Brady never boasted about it, and the rest of the kids had a healthy sense of humor regarding it. There were no perks with this made-up title, but I believe that it influenced a higher sense of accountability in Brady. It helped a middle child feel a little bigger.

Accountability and Expectations

Brady has great observation skills. I first noted how acute they were with the water experiment test. When the kids were young, I'd show them a tall, thin glass and a wide, short glass. I filled a measuring cup with one cup of water. They'd watch as I poured it into the tall glass. I filled the measuring cup with another cup of water and poured it into the short glass. I'd ask which glass had more water. The answer was *the tall one*— until Brady came along and said, "Actually they have the same amount. They only look different." I spontaneously shouted, "Brady, you're a genius!" He had a spark in his eyes when I said it, and I watched him smile and pause. I knew he had listened to what I had said and was considering if it were true. I knew it was worth reinforcing. He loved numbers and counting. I gave him the job of counting everything. I'd spill a large box of paper clips and let him count them. He would stay on task until every clip was counted and returned to the box. He thought it was fun. I knew he believed me when I called him a genius that day, and he was just acting accountably as one himself.

Accountability in School

Brady loved school and loved playing with his friends. At my children's elementary school, recess was fifteen minutes of a thirty-minute lunch break. Their school had strict rules about no talking in class, staying single file while walking, and wearing proper uniforms, with shirts always tucked in. It was strange to see such playful boys look so serious going to school. They looked like they were going to the office, wearing suit coats and ties as they got out of the car at drop-off. It's no wonder that a third-grader who's forced to sit in a hot classroom wearing a man's suit for hours at a time looks forward to the outdoor freedom of recess.

Kids inhaled the contents of their lunches and raced outside at the sound of the old-fashioned schoolhouse handbell. The kids rushed out the back door to the lot behind the school, abandoning their ties, suit jackets, and sense of order along the way. The teachers and administrators considered the fifteen minutes of pure bedlam necessary for discharging the pent-up energy. Losing the privilege of recess and being forced to stay in an empty classroom listening to the fun and giggles of your classmates from the open windows was a grave punishment.

My kids were pretty well behaved. When I was asked to visit Miss Curley's classroom after school, I never considered that it would be to discuss a problem. Miss Curley was the third-grade teacher. She had a reputation for being strict, and most of the kids at the school were afraid of her. She believed in timed math tests and was a stickler for following directions, but I thought she was fair. Both Adam and Tyler had Miss Curley without any issues. One day, she called me in to discuss Brady, who was her student at that time. It was after the first marking period, and she had Brady's report card on her desk when I got there. Brady was an exceptional student. I assumed that she'd called me in to suggest adding more advanced work to my eight-year-old sanctioned genius's schedule. I guessed wrong.

She thanked me for coming in and asked me to sit down. She handed me the report card and asked if it was my signature on the back. I thought it was a peculiar question. I acknowledged that the signature was mine. Then she reached behind her desk and handed me a stack of Brady's tests. The tests were mostly marked with 100 percent at the top of the pages. The lowest grade I noticed was marked 95 percent. I was confused. I thought she couldn't possibly take issue with Brady not getting all perfect grades. It made no sense.

Then she pointed to the signatures on the tests—all of them. They were identical to each other but not even close to my signature on his report card. It began to make sense. She asked me what I thought. I paused to think.

THE INFLUENCE OF ACCOUNTABILITY

When our kids are dishonest, it's important to stay neutral and listen for facts. It can be disappointing, but if you jump to conclusions before you know what actually happened, you can sink even deeper into disappointment when the truth is revealed.

"I think Brady either signed them himself or asked someone to sign them for him, that's what I think. But why have someone else sign tests with great grades?" I said in response, with even greater confusion.

"Brady is an outstanding student, but it looks like he forged your signature, and that is against our school code. He signed your name more than a dozen times. He is going to lose his privileges. I am forced to restrict his recess for at least two weeks," she explained reluctantly.

I told her that I understood that she needed to address this with Brady and that I, too, planned to have a conversation with him about his dishonesty and my expectations of him going forward. I thanked her as I left the classroom. Some saw Miss Curley as strict and inflexible. I liked her because she believed in accountability.

Personal Accountability

When I got home, Brady was waiting for me with a sad, guilty face. I walked toward him and asked if he knew why I was called to his teacher's classroom. He reluctantly nodded yes. I asked him why he would sign my name.

He began his explanation with, "You were busy—"

I signaled by waving my "stop" hand and interrupted him abruptly. "Ah, ah, ah. Stop. Try again. I had nothing to do with you making the decision to sign my name," I said firmly.

"I'm just saying"—he continued in a panic—"I was afraid I would lose recess if I handed my test in without a signature, and then I realized when I got my second test that the signatures needed to match, so I thought I better just keep signing your name. But the first time you were busy, Mom."

I looked directly at him and asked him in a calm voice, "Are you saying that I was too busy for you? Are you saying that I was too busy doing something that was more important than your school needs? Because if that is what you're saying, that is an entirely different conversation. This conversation isn't about discussing my shortcomings as your mother; it is about your dishonesty as a son and as a student."

He began to cry.

One thing I was consistent about was refusing to *share* the blame with my kids for their mistakes. Forgery wasn't both of our faults. It was entirely his fault. That sounds harsh, but I knew the only way for my children to develop their power to make solid decisions was to hold them accountable. I didn't bail them out, negotiate with teachers, or make excuses. It was difficult for me to watch them miss opportunities because they forgot permission slips or get points taken off of a project because they turned it in late. That is part of being a parent.

Accountable Kids Are Still Kids

Some parents give in to the temptation to cover up their kids' mistakes because they fear that people will assign it as their—the parents'—mistake, not their kids'. Kids are supposed to make mistakes and learn from them. If we as parents erase their mistakes, we erase their opportunity to learn

THE INFLUENCE OF ACCOUNTABILITY

from them. When they learn from a mistake and they have the awareness and self-control not to repeat it, their confidence jumps. It took a lot of foresight for an eight-year-old to know that he had to keep the test signatures consistent. The fear that he would lose his recess time for turning in an unsigned test pushed him into taking a dishonest action. I gave him time to think about the possible consequences that each of the choices he had made may have caused. He sat with me and thoughtfully shared his impressions. He said he would have lost one day of recess if he'd told Miss Curley that he forgot to have his test signed. But he realized that by forging my signature and continuing it for weeks, the punishment would be much more severe. We also talked about the way he felt getting caught in a lie.

"I feel terrible. I feel like you're mad at me," he said, fighting tears.

"I'm not mad at you," I said consolingly. "I feel badly that you didn't think a problem through and rushed to fix it by lying, then tried to blame me for it. You know you will face consequences for this."

"I know. I'm probably going to lose my recess," he said.

"I imagine you will, but that's the consequence the school will give you. I have my own penalty that you will have to face." His eyes widened, and he looked up at me as I explained. "I'm going to think about it and tell you after dinner."

"I'm really sorry, Mommy," he said, crying.

"I believe that you are sorry. But I expect you to do more than tell me you're sorry. I expect you to show me you're sorry. We'll talk about it after dinner." I left the room. It's important to walk away and give your child a clear signal that there is zero opportunity for them to negotiate what the next step will be. Full stop.

> Too much time is wasted in parenting listening
> to endless apologies formed in words instead of
> seeing the apologies carried out in actions.

Accountability and Punishments

The school's penalties differed from mine. The school's policy was to take things away as a punishment. My penalties added more work as a learning rehabilitation instead of a sacrificing punishment. I knew that Brady was very resourceful, and that can work against a person if they don't have foresight. A resourceful person can think quickly on their feet, but a young resourceful person lacks the experience to anticipate the consequences of a quick decision. That's where Brady was. At the tender age of eight, he was more a problem solver than a strategist. He thought quickly about what needed to be done to keep his recess, so he signed the test himself. He had no plan beyond that. When the second test was given to him, he knew he would get caught in his forgery scam if the signatures didn't match. So, he signed it again, and again.

After dinner that night, I handed Brady a book titled, *What Your Fourth Grader Needs to Know*. It was a 389-page comprehensive curriculum book that included language arts, history, math, fine arts, and science, designed to give a fourth-grade student a leg up. I had dozens of school workbooks and course books for the kids. I'd have them complete work in them during the summer to earn time to use the computer or play video games. I'd seen this comprehensive series when I was buying books for Adam months earlier, when he started his first homeschool year. I had been saving it for the summer, but this seemed to be the perfect opportunity to open it up.

"What's this for? I'm in third grade," he said as he flipped through the book that clearly said fourth grade. I handed him a fresh wide-ruled spiral notebook and explained, "I thought since you forged my signature, practicing cursive writing would be a perfect task for you to undertake."

He seemed relieved and asked, "Okay, what pages do you want me to write out?"

"All of them," I said. "I am sure that you will finish before fourth grade, and you will be the most prepared student in class next year." I turned to walk away.

He started to cry and protested that he would never be able to finish rewriting the entire book. I told him he was underestimating himself and asked him whether, at the beginning of the school year, he would've imagined it possible to forge my name on his tests for an entire semester without it being detected. I clarified that forging my signature was a serious violation and even a crime. Using a pen is a privilege, and I told him I was offering him that privilege every day until the entire book was transcribed.

He took the book and the notebook from me. The house was silent. I had a no-nonsense mothering reputation, especially when it came to blaming others. The kids knew I wasn't interested in excuses. His older brothers pleaded for leniency and said they feared his hand might fall off. I knew better, but I appreciated how the kids supported each other.

Accountability Lessons

Brady spent the winter filling notebook after notebook. He added a few pages each day and budgeted his time well, still having room for television, playing in the snow, and challenging his brothers at video games. In early spring, he asked me to buy him more spiral notebooks. I knew he had already rewritten nearly three hundred pages, so I offered clemency and told him that he'd done a great job and didn't have to finish the whole book. He told me that he wanted to. He said he had less than one hundred pages left and wanted to finish it. I got him more notebooks.

It's important to offer kids a chance to learn something new by integrating something different. If I had grounded him or taken away TV or computer privileges, he'd be wrestling with his own thoughts. It was his own thoughts that had gotten him into trouble. I wanted him to take in more ideas, new ideas. I was banking on the belief that the task of transcribing the knowledge of Alexander the Great, Isaac Newton, and Sojourner Truth would expose Brady to fresh strategies. I tailored this master plan to serve him and the specific situation, so that Brady could eventually manage it as his personal project.

Being Thankful for Accountability

Some kids are intellectually curious; they question the *what* in a situation. Other kids are emotionally curious; they want to know *why* something happened. But Brady was a physically curious child. He had a kinetic curiosity about how things worked. His curiosity got the best of him during Thanksgiving dinner preparations one year when he was eleven. I had run to the store to get something last minute. When I returned twenty minutes later, I found sawed hash marks on the edge of the countertop near the stove. I noticed the electric knife in close proximity and what looked like sawdust on the floor. I was not the listed genius in my family, but I was able to piece this experimental crime scene together.

"Who cut up the counter with the electric knife?" I screamed, receiving no response. "Fine. I will just compare my files against the fingerprints, which I am sure the wannabe lumberjack left on his electric ax."

This may sound ridiculous (no, it *is* ridiculous), but this was a lever I used on occasion to prevent the temptation of the kids to lie. It was my figurative fence that prevented them from falling into a pool of lies. I thought of the idea out of necessity. When you have a bunch of kids close together in age, they cover for each other and share blame for each other. That's supportive but dishonest. As mentioned previously, I believe in creative rehabilitation, not sacrificing punishments. For it to be effective, it must be tailored to the action and the person. When the boys were very young, they all confessed to writing on the bathroom cabinet with nail polish. It happened while I was in the hospital having their sister, Jordan. Their dad told them that I would talk to them about it when I got home. When I got home, I unpacked papers from the hospital to put them in a safe place, and they noticed the sheet with Jordan's footprints. They asked if they could see the paper and if it was really her footprints.

An idea was born. I said, "Yes, they are her real footprints. I was given a sheet like this when each of you were born. I have your fingerprints too. They're in a file upstairs. I am going to use them to figure out who was playing with the nail polish by comparing the fingerprints." It was a stretch, but they looked at each other, and I knew they believed that, somehow, I had this forensic power.

It worked. About fifteen minutes later, Adam made a full confession. The kids never questioned my access to their fingerprints or skill of reading them. I would interject from time to time, "Don't worry about tattling; I'll just get the fingerprints." Or, I would hear them warn each other, "She's got the fingerprints."

So, when I said I would let the fingerprints do the talking that choppy Thanksgiving Day, I meant it. Brady was still young enough to believe me and confessed. He said he couldn't help himself. He wanted to know if the knife was sharp enough to cut wood. I was furious. I was angry that he had been so careless. I was a little rattled that his carelessness could have hurt him or someone else.

"You were curious? So, you ignored all consequences and just cut up the counter?" I asked.

"Well, I did think about it. The blades are locked, and it was totally safe. I didn't think the marks would be that noticeable. It was an experiment," he explained.

"Experiment? Now you're a scientist? What step in the scientific method says, 'Forget logic and do whatever you want'? No step, that's what step!" I replied with frustration.

"I can fix it, Mom," he said.

My Thanksgiving tirade began.

"Fix it? Do you think I want a fifth-grader repairing my counter? I don't think so. I want a new countertop. I don't want an easy-to-saw-up Formica counter. I want a sturdy and durable granite countertop. And guess what? It's more than you can afford right now. Do you know what that means? Every time you look at this counter, it's going to remind you to study very hard so you can go to a good college and get an excellent job so you can have it replaced properly. Do you understand?"

Brady nodded yes. Forty minutes later, we all assembled around the dining room table. He offered in our premeal gratitude prayer chain that he was grateful that no one got hurt when he was fooling around with the electric knife. I was grateful too; it was a thankful Thanksgiving.

The Benefits of Accountability

Fifteen years later, Brady and I sat at a restaurant in Morningside Heights in New York City celebrating his graduation from Columbia University the day before. Brady had studied physics as an undergraduate, studied abroad, and completed his master's degree in biostatistics. He became an actual scientist. I was writing this book at the time, so I stayed an extra day to talk about some of his strongest childhood memories. He told me that it always amazed him that I never seemed to worry about him or the other kids being angry at me. He said he was grateful that I never tried to be his friend and that it gave me a higher standing in his eyes.

We talked about his book transcription punishment in third grade. He shared with me why he decided to transcribe the entire book, even after I told him he could stop. He said he wanted to prove to himself, and to me, that he could copy the whole book. When he did it, and it was his choice, it gave him confidence. Allowing our kids to manage their own consequences can help them gain confidence in holding themselves accountable. I learned how valuable that was from an adult Brady sharing his impressions that day over dinner.

After we left the restaurant and started walking back to his apartment, Brady stopped, turned to me, and said, "Mom, I've been thinking. Pretty soon I hope to be able to replace that countertop. Do you want to pick it out, or do you want me to surprise you and have it done while you're away somewhere?"

I wrote on our porch that Brady was a genius the summer before his forgery scam.

Being a genius isn't determined by what you know.
It's about being accountable for what you know.

Brady was able to understand the difference. He developed the influence of accountability.

Establishing Accountability

Set boundaries for behavior, and be consistent in enforcing them. If something is off-limits, it's off-limits. Eliminate arbitrary adjustments for the sake of convenience. Predictability is safe. If you have ever wondered why your young child wants to watch *Beauty and the Beast* repeatedly, it is because they can anticipate what is coming next through the repetition of watching it so many times. They get to warn you, "This is the part where..." It gives them power. Be consistent, and they will understand that consequence isn't arbitrary. They will feel more powerful and capable of making the right choice and coping with restrictions.

Start setting limits and expectations early, and communicate instructions plainly. Don't leave room for assumptions. Ask them if they understand why the rule restricts something. Make sure that your rules travel with them. What they are allowed to do at home should be the same as at their friend's house.

Make consequences clear and rewards clearer. Make an intentional, specific comment about behavior they engaged in that was responsible. Being told we're responsible, and then having it attached to evidence of our actions, makes a deeper, more believable impression and sets us up for positive self-talk. If we hold a core belief that we are responsible, we are more likely to act responsibly. Create a culture of accountability, and you'll raise kids who respond without blame, excuses, or buts. We use the influence of accountability not to make our lives easier as parents but to help our kids live a life that's more fulfilling. When our kids learn to hold themselves accountable, it serves everyone they love.

CHAPTER 10
The Influence of Kindness

KIND·NESS

/ˈkīn(d)nəs/

noun

the quality of being friendly, generous, and considerate

Synonyms: considerateness, compassion, selflessness

Antonyms: unkindness, selfishness, meaninglessness

Kindness is the connective tissue that structures our integrity. It reveals who we are at our very core, how we act when no one is watching. When kids catch parents in a moment of doing the right thing, it's powerful. But it's more than a matter of adding credibility. Kindness is credible because it confirms the effectiveness of doing the right thing. It's powerful because it's real life, in real time. Practiced over time, it demonstrates right from wrong and helps kids develop a healthy inner voice. Having an inner voice influenced by kindness develops strong character.

In the popular fairy tale *Pinocchio*, the would-be boy had Jiminy Cricket to explain moral ethics. He said that temptations are the wrong things that seem right at the time. Real people don't have a wise, gentlemanly insect to guide them; they must rely on their conscience. Our conscience is the unseen persuader in our behavior. It's also important to incorporate empathy and compassion in order to develop a sense of right and wrong.

Kindness Withholds Judgment

Remember when landline phones were a thing? If your house was anything like mine before cell phones took over the world, it was common to get frequent calls from telemarketers. When they'd call, I had a regular script that I'd follow.

"Yes, this is Kelly," I would answer. Then after a minute of hearing them out, I would say, "I appreciate the offer, but I don't take solicitations over the phone. Have a great night and good luck." It only took a few seconds, and it was my usual habit of handling telemarketers.

One evening during one of those disruptive calls, I offered my regular script to the telemarketer and didn't realize that my daughter Jordan was standing behind me. She was about ten at the time. After I hung up the phone, she asked me why I didn't just say that I wasn't home. I told her I didn't say that because I *was* home. She suggested that next time, maybe she should answer the phone and tell them I was in the shower and couldn't come to the phone. It became clear to me after she offered this advice that she had seen someone else handle telemarketers differently. I asked her whether, if she told the caller that I was in the shower when I wasn't, it would be a lie. She thought for a few seconds and said it wouldn't be a *real* lie. This surprised me, because Jordan was an incredibly thoughtful child, and I was confident that she knew right from wrong, so I kept quizzing her.

"What is a real lie?" I asked.

"A real lie is when you say something that is made up to someone you know."

The more she tried to explain, the more I understood that she had a disconnect in her understanding of truth and lies. She continued to explain that when she was at her friend Courtney's house, her mom asked Courtney to answer the phone and, if it was someone calling to sell something, to say that she was giving the baby a bath.

"Telemarketers are so annoying," she added as she finished the story.

Witnessing your son or daughter repeat dishonest behavior that they learned outside your home feels like a numbing kick in the gut. Stunned, I turned to her and asked, "What do you mean, annoying?" This phrase seemed so unlike anything I'd ever expect her to say. She struggled to put it into words and finally admitted that she didn't know. I asked her if she knew what a telemarketer was. She said she didn't know that either.

Show Kindness to Strangers

Seeing the effects of negative influence is distressing. And no matter if it's your first or tenth encounter, it's always frustrating. The truth is, even when a parent models thoughtful behaviors to be a positive influence, we can sometimes get out-influenced. When this happens, a parent becomes Jiminy Cricket and helps the child rethink, to see that the actions they thought to be so right were actually so wrong. I found that

asking thoughtful questions instead of lecturing worked best when helping one of my kids unlearn a bad behavior.

I sat with Jordan on the couch to start the process of unlearning. I
asked her what a lie was. She told me that it's when you say something
that isn't true.

I asked, "If you told someone you didn't know something that wasn't
true, would that be a lie?"

Jordan has an incredibly kind nature and sees the best in people,
sometimes to a fault.

She paused and said, "I don't know."

I could see doubt creeping in. I seized the opportunity and asked
her if she thought some people deserved to be told the truth and some
people didn't.

She said no without hesitation. Then I asked her if she wanted to
know what a telemarketer was. She seemed curious, so I explained that a
telemarketer was a person who had the job of calling people on a list to
ask them if they wanted to buy something that the company they worked
for was selling. It was their job that they got a paycheck for, so they
could buy food and have a place to live. She seemed surprised. Her eyes
started to tear up. I told her that it's important to tell the truth because
we deserve to be honest people. The things we do show who we are. It
doesn't matter if we are speaking to a stranger or a friend, what we say
and how we say it shows what *we* are about.

I had no control over the rules in Courtney's house. When negative influencers swayed behavior like this, I tried to pull the attention
back to my kids and who they wanted to be, instead of focusing on who
others were. It's unproductive to spend time inventorying what's wrong

with someone else or something else, rather than focusing on what is right with *us* and how *we* can improve. Ideally, that's the way kindness should work.

Kindness Finds Commonality

Kindness is rooted in compassion. Before my mother moved to Florida, Jordan would visit her grandmother after school. They would talk about Jordan's day, go for a walk, have a snack, and watch reruns of *M*A*S*H*, *Gunsmoke*, and *The Golden Girls*. My mother loved the company. Some days Jordan would read poetry, practice her oratory piece for speech and debate competitions for my mom and the people in her apartment complex, or set up a night of entertainment for the residents. Jordan was so comfortable around people seventy years her senior. Actually, she made everyone in her company feel comfortable. People walked away from a conversation with Jordan feeling better about themselves. They still do.

> **That's what happens when a person acts from a point of kindness: they see commonalities, not differences.**

Kindness Is Honest

When Jordan was very young, she had a serious illness. She suffered high fevers that impaired her speech, sight, and sensory processing. She had to learn how to walk for a second time. She had to practice fine motor skills and get used to textures, tastes, and smells all over again. It was frustrating for her. She was still speech delayed by the time she began first grade and continued speech therapy for the next eight years. I sent her to the same school her brothers were attending. It was small and had limited learning support. I was newly divorced, and that was a big adjustment for all the kids. I didn't want Jordan to also experience a different school from her siblings.

My experience teaching adults and college students taught me that it works against kids when they are labeled with limits on their learning abilities early in their school life and that it ends up having a lifelong effect on how they look at their own intellectual capacity. It was a challenge as a teacher to help my students reengineer core beliefs that were false. They were convinced that they didn't have a math brain or couldn't gain reading comprehension skills. They'd had the wrong support, which limited their playing field instead of leveling it. Creating safeguards that prevent kids from failing can set limits and overcompensate for their learning differences. They can get too bored if they're not challenged. It can prevent them from exploring passions. I didn't want to make that mistake with Jordan by transferring her to the public school for segregated learning support outside of a traditional classroom. She was delayed, not impaired. I knew she would catch up, but I also knew it wasn't going to be easy for her.

She has dyslexia, and thus she had difficulties with learning to read, concentrating, and following multistep directions. But it's a misunderstanding to think that dyslexic people see the page backward, like a mirror image. That isn't how Jordan described it. She said the letters or words would dance around on the page, like they couldn't stay still. Amazingly, she was able to keep it together during the school day. Her teachers trusted that she could finish her work after school with me, in addition to her homework. The school pushed back after third grade, however, when the reading list became more demanding. The summer reading list for fourth grade included six books, and they were mandatory. They felt that the list might be too much for her. I never took their discouragement seriously.

The Impact of Kindness

Sometimes being kind isn't simply agreeing and going along with something. Sometimes it's telling people to be careful and rethink something, or it's pointing out the pitfalls. The school was being kind to me. I felt that her teachers were offering more of a warning than a disapproval. We were able to find some books on cassette or CD at the library, and some of her brothers, her younger sister, and I took turns reading to her from a second copy as she followed along. I never had a conversation with Jordan about her learning disabilities. She knew there was something different about her, but I didn't want her to think that unusual was abnormal. Because it isn't. I explained that we all learn differently, and schools used the most common way to teach lessons.

It was awkward at first for her to listen and follow along. It was awkward for her siblings to be promoted to lecturers in chief, but after the first few days, it became a family project. Brady calculated how many hours per day we'd need to complete the books in time. We kept a chart on the refrigerator, and Jordan started to manage the schedule of the daily *actors* who would read to her. She made big strides that summer. We noticed that she could memorize long sections of the book and that she could remember the exact pages we left off at. This would prove to be a valuable skill for her.

Kindness Is Humble

She returned to school in September well prepared and full of confidence. Her teachers were impressed with her progress, and during the second quarter, they asked for a meeting. They suggested including a word bank on her reading tests that was fill-in-the-blank style, so that Jordan could focus, without her mind wandering, and finish the test on time. The word bank the teacher provided was a list of twenty vocabulary words without definitions that were covered in the lesson. The teacher explained that many of the kids found it helpful. It made a big difference. Jordan wasn't the only student in the class who used a word bank, but she was the only one of those students who made the honor roll that semester.

We have a local paper in my town that publishes an edition once a week on Wednesdays. It includes the school honor rolls, listing each child alphabetically by grade. One day Jordan's teacher asked me to come to school to talk. When I got to the school, I saw the mother of one of her classmates in the parking lot. She asked me not to be upset and try to understand why she was asking the school to make two honor rolls. I had no idea what she was talking about. She continued pleading her case that it wasn't fair that her daughter took the same tests my daughter did without a word bank. She believed that Jordan had an unfair advantage, and because of this extra help, she shouldn't be listed on the *real* honor roll. It started to become clear to me why I had been called to the school. She said she'd recommended that the newspaper use asterisks on the honor roll to mark the names of those students who used accommodations on tests. I didn't respond to her. I just blinked and thought how lucky I was not to be her.

The Circles of Kindness

I walked into the school and found Jordan's teacher. I told her what had happened in the parking lot. She shared that she did not know how anyone found out that Jordan used a word bank and was sorry that some of the parents felt threatened by it. She said it was ridiculous and that, going forward, every student would have a word bank on their test. She confirmed that Jordan had earned every grade and that the word bank just organized the material for her. That teacher performed an act of kindness. Like a magic loop, it circled back to Jordan. Jordan's teacher, her siblings, me—we all learned from her. Jordan taught us that a teacher's goal isn't to transfer information from a book to a student. Master teachers help their students transform information and make it accessible and comfortable.

Jordan went on to merit her place on the honor roll throughout high school, and she used her uncanny memorization skills to become a national competitor in the Forensics Speech and Debate League. She loved it so much that she majored in theater in college and graduated with honors. Presently, she attends one of the top graduate schools in the country, CalArts. She is working toward her MFA in creative production and stage management. Basically, she creates a schedule for actors to read aloud from their scripts as she follows along in her book. Life circles back.

Kindness offers a happy ending to any story.

Kindness Is an Opportunity

Kindness is more than caring about others; it's an opportunity to affirm who we really are at our very core. Offering an unprompted gesture without expecting anything in return is what kindness is about. My youngest daughter, Dagny, got that opportunity in mid-2018, after the Olympics, *Dancing with the Stars*, and Brady's graduation from Columbia, when each day seemed more awesome than the day before. Shockingly, I suffered a terrible accident. I fell and hit my head on the pavement and ended up with multiple facial injuries. It happened while I was working out of town. After a day at the hospital and an overnight stay with a relative, I came home to a hero's welcome. I couldn't work for several weeks. After all, who wants to listen to a motivational speaker with two black eyes and a gaping hole above her nose? About a month later, there was an event I'd committed to working that I couldn't cancel. It was three days of presenting six-hour seminars outside of Pittsburgh. I was very nervous about my facial injuries, the long drive, and having the stamina to keep my wits about me and be prepared. That's when Dagny revealed who she was at her core. She quieted my anxiety with kindness. Kindness is more than telling someone that everything will be okay—it's actively engaging with them to *make* everything okay.

First, she offered me my first lesson in full coverage make-up application. It was exactly what I needed to help cover some of the injuries and bruising that remained. Next, she cleared her schedule and drove with me on the five-hour ride to Pittsburgh. Once we arrived on-site, she helped me prepare notes. She gently but succinctly told me what I needed to do about ten minutes before I needed to do it. Dagny had never come to work with me, not even on Take Your Child to Work Day, but she instinctively knew what to do. Dressed for success, my nineteen-year-old daughter took a clipboard and covered for me as she interacted with people during the breaks, allowing me time to rest. She